SpringerBriefs in Computer Science

SpringerBriefs present concise summaries of cutting-edge research and practical applications across a wide spectrum of fields. Featuring compact volumes of 50 to 125 pages, the series covers a range of content from professional to academic.

Typical topics might include:

- A timely report of state-of-the art analytical techniques
- A bridge between new research results, as published in journal articles, and a contextual literature review
- A snapshot of a hot or emerging topic
- An in-depth case study or clinical example
- A presentation of core concepts that students must understand in order to make independent contributions

Briefs allow authors to present their ideas and readers to absorb them with minimal time investment. Briefs will be published as part of Springer's eBook collection, with millions of users worldwide. In addition, Briefs will be available for individual print and electronic purchase. Briefs are characterized by fast, global electronic dissemination, standard publishing contracts, easy-to-use manuscript preparation and formatting guidelines, and expedited production schedules. We aim for publication 8–12 weeks after acceptance. Both solicited and unsolicited manuscripts are considered for publication in this series.

**Indexing: This series is indexed in Scopus, Ei-Compendex, and zbMATH **

Hamed Tabrizchi • Ali Aghasi

Federated Cyber Intelligence

Federated Learning for Cybersecurity

 Springer

Hamed Tabrizchi
Department of Computer Science, Faculty
of Mathematics, Statistics, and
Computer Science
University of Tabriz
Tabriz, Iran

Ali Aghasi
Faculty of Computer Engineering
University of Isfahan
Isfahan, Iran

ISSN 2191-5768   ISSN 2191-5776   (electronic)
SpringerBriefs in Computer Science
ISBN 978-3-031-86591-6   ISBN 978-3-031-86592-3   (eBook)
https://doi.org/10.1007/978-3-031-86592-3

This Springer imprint is published by the registered company Springer Nature Switzerland AG
The registered company address is: Gewerbestrasse 11, 6330 Cham, Switzerland

If disposing of this product, please recycle the paper.

Preface

The rapid growth of cybersecurity risks, with the growing need to safeguard data privacy, has led to the development of novel solutions that enable cooperation while ensuring secrecy. Federated learning is a novel methodology that facilitates decentralized learning while preserving data integrity. This book, *Federated Cyber Intelligence*, examines the intersection between federated learning and cybersecurity. Upon completing this book, readers will grasp its core concepts, their practical uses, and potential applications.

This book starts with Chapter 1, which explains the fundamental ideas of federated learning. Chapter 2 elucidates the essential methodological and technical components of federated learning. Chapter 3 pertains to cybersecurity, providing essential insights into the principles, challenges, and evolving landscape of cyber defense. Chapter 4 analyzes the impact of federated learning on modern cybersecurity systems. It demonstrates its capacity to identify and alleviate dangers using decentralized intelligence. Chapter 5 ultimately contemplates the insights acquired and analyzes the forthcoming trajectory, emphasizing future problems and possibilities in federated cyber intelligence.

This book is intended for scholars and educators aiming to comprehend the relationship between federated learning and cybersecurity.

Tabriz, Iran
Isfahan, Iran

Hamed Tabrizchi
Ali Aghasi

Contents

Chapter 1
Introduction to Federated Learning

1.1 Introduction

In an era where data is more valuable than gold, the protection and ethical use of data have become essential. With FL, a whole new way of analyzing data has opened up, promising a new paradigm for privacy, security, and collaboration. Federated learning is a machine learning setting, in which the goal is to train a model across a variety of decentralized devices or servers that contain local data samples, without exchanging them. Thus, many privacy and security concerns inherent in traditional machine learning models can be addressed without ever centralizing data. Moreover, the field of communication and networking is eagerly seeking machine learning-based decision-making solutions. These are seen as a replacement for the traditional model-driven methods, which have been found inadequate in capturing the increasing complexity and diversity of contemporary systems in the field. On the other hand, traditional machine learning solutions typically rely on central entities, often cloud-based, to process data. However, the challenges associated with accessing private data and the substantial costs of transmitting raw data to the central entity have led to the emergence of a decentralized machine learning method known as Federated Learning [1, 2].

Federated learning was developed in response to the requirement to make use of the enormous amount of data that is generated every day across a wide range of devices, such as smartphones and Internet of Things devices while respecting the security and right to privacy of the user. Traditional machine learning approaches require centralized data storage, which poses significant privacy risks and logistical challenges. Federated learning, on the other hand, allows a model to be trained across multiple devices by using their computational resources and data without moving the data itself. Aside from addressing privacy concerns, this new training paradigm also offers new opportunities for collaborative intelligence across diverse sectors and entities [2].

© The Author(s), under exclusive license to Springer Nature
Switzerland AG 2025
H. Tabrizchi, A. Aghasi, *Federated Cyber Intelligence*, SpringerBriefs in
Computer Science, https://doi.org/10.1007/978-3-031-86592-3_1

1.2   The Shift from Centralized to Decentralized Learning

As a result of the shift from centralized to decentralized learning, a revolutionary paradigm transition has occurred in the fields of machine learning and data processing. Traditionally, centralized learning relied on aggregating data from multiple sources into a single, central repository where models were trained. This approach, while effective in terms of data availability and model performance, raised significant concerns related to scalability, data privacy, security, and compliance with regulatory standards. Decentralized learning provided by federated learning addresses these concerns by enabling model training across distributed data sources without necessitating data transfer to a central location. Besides mitigating privacy risks, this transition also facilitates scalable and efficient data utilization, enhancing collaboration across industries and maintaining data ownership [2].

1.2.1   Decentralized vs Distributed

This centralized approach to machine learning has been the standard for many years. It has been used in a wide range of applications, from predictive analytics in business to image recognition in computer vision. The strength of this approach lies in its ability to leverage powerful central processing units (CPUs) and graphics processing units (GPUs), often housed in data centers, to crunch large volumes of data. However, this model is not without its drawbacks. The transmission of data from local storage to the central hub can be costly, both in terms of time and resources. It also raises privacy concerns, as sensitive data must leave its local environment. Furthermore, the centralized model can create a bottleneck, where the speed of learning is limited by the processing power of the central hub. In response to these challenges, the field of machine learning has begun to explore decentralized approaches. These new methods aim to distribute the learning process across multiple nodes, reducing the need for data transmission and alleviating the processing bottleneck. This shift in paradigm opens up exciting new possibilities for machine learning, promising to revolutionize the field in the years to come [3].

To achieve greater transparency, it is necessary to distinguish between decentralization and distribution. The terms "decentralized" and "distributed" are often used interchangeably in the context of data processing, but they have distinct meanings and implications. It is essential to understand these differences to understand the nature of federated learning and its role in modern data science [3, 4].

- **Distributed learning** involves splitting the learning task across multiple nodes, which work in parallel to process and compute different parts of the data. This method improves computation and model training, making it particularly effective for handling large datasets and complex models. However, it often requires a central coordinator to coordinate tasks and aggregate results. This can create a bottleneck and pose a single point of failure.

- **Decentralized learning** eliminates the need for a central authority by distributing the learning process across multiple nodes that independently process their local data. Each node contributes to the global model by sharing only model updates rather than raw data. This approach enhances data privacy and security, as sensitive information remains on local devices. Decentralized learning is especially useful in scenarios where data privacy is crucial. In addition to managing the overhead of communication, it may face challenges in ensuring consistent and efficient model updates across all nodes.

Federated learning can be viewed as a specific form of decentralized learning. In FL, multiple clients (such as mobile devices or organizations) collaboratively train a model under the orchestration of a central server, but unlike traditional distributed learning, the clients' raw data is never transferred to the server. Instead, only model updates are shared, which are then aggregated to improve the global model. This unique approach ensures data privacy and security while enhancing collaborative learning. Table 1.1 illustrates the key differences between decentralized and distributed learning.

In summary, while both decentralized and distributed learning involves multiple nodes working together, federated learning is inherently decentralized, to protect data privacy and security while only sharing model updates. As a result of this distinction, it is possible to better understand the innovative approach and advantages offered by federated learning in a variety of applications.

1.3   Federated Learning: Definitions, Preliminaries, and General Concept

Federated learning represents a significant shift towards more privacy-conscious and efficient machine learning models, particularly valuable in fields where data sensitivity and privacy are paramount. In the following subsections, our first chapter explores the definitions, preliminaries, and general concepts of Federated learning. Beginning with a foundational overview, this section introduces the advanced learning paradigm of federated learning. It is followed by a general explanation of the essential concepts and requirements, ensuring readers acquire a comprehensive understanding of the background knowledge. The exploration concludes by defining the general concept of federated learning, offering a brief overview of its

Table 1.1 Key differences between decentralized and distributed learning

Factors	Decentralized learning	Distributed learning
Data location	Data remains on local nodes	Data can be split and shared across nodes
Privacy	High, since data stays local	Varies, data may be shared
Scalability	High, nodes operate independently	High, but dependent on a central server
Use cases	Privacy-sensitive applications	Large-scale data and complex models

functionality, significance in machine learning, and its impactful implications for privacy and data decentralization in computational models.

1.3.1   Definitions

In any field of study, grasping the fundamental terms is essential. Attempting to comprehend the core principles without this foundation can prove unproductive. In this context, we present the pivotal terms that form the backbone of federated learning [5, 6].

- Machine learning (ML): Machine learning is a subset of artificial intelligence (AI) that enables computers to learn and make decisions from data without being explicitly programmed for specific tasks, by identifying patterns and making predictions or decisions based on input data.
- Federated Learning: Federated learning is an ML paradigm that enables collaborative model training by multiple entities without centralizing raw data, maintaining privacy and reducing data transmission costs through local training and central aggregation of model updates.
- Central Server: In FL, a central server orchestrates the learning process, aggregating model updates from participating clients to update a global model.
- Client: An entity, such as a mobile phone or an organization, that participates in FL by training models on local data and sending model updates to the central server.
- Global Model: The aggregated model is updated by the central server in FL, which is subsequently shared with clients for further local training rounds.
- Local Model: The model trained by clients on their local data in the context of FL.

1.3.2   Preliminaries

Understanding the complexities of federated learning requires delving into the foundational principles that distinguish it from traditional machine learning paradigms. This exploration begins by addressing three core principles: Privacy Preservation, Decentralization, and Data Heterogeneity [6].

1.3.2.1   Privacy Preservation

In an era in which data breaches and unauthorized access to data are of great concern, FL offers the principle that suits privacy preservation. With this principle, clients can contribute to the development of sophisticated machine-learning models while retaining their data locally. This means that personal or sensitive information does not pass through the network or get stored on a centralized server. Therefore, FL inherently reduces the attack surface for potential data breaches, making it a better choice for industries where data sensitivity is non-negotiable, such as healthcare, finance, and personal services. It is worth reminding that this book is not about the security of FL but is about the potential contributions of FL to the cyber securities era.

1.3.2.2 Decentralization

Decentralization is another essential concept of federated learning. To process and analyze data from various sources, traditional machine learning methodologies rely heavily on central data repositories. The centralized approach not only presents significant privacy risks but also becomes a bottleneck for scalability and presents challenges in managing and securing large amounts of data. As a distributed learning approach, FL focuses on decentralizing the learning process across several clients. The client computes its data and shares only model updates-such as weights or gradients-with the server. The paradigm shift not only mitigates the risk of centralized data breaches but also democratizes the learning process, enabling devices and entities to actively contribute to model development.

1.3.2.3 Data Heterogeneity

Federated learning is characterized by the inherent heterogeneity of the data among the participating clients. Before training, datasets are often homogenized and carefully curated in traditional settings. Despite this, FL operates under the assumption that real-world data is messy, diverse, and unbalanced. Across clients, data may not be independently and identically distributed, which means that the distribution of data may vary significantly from one client to another. As an example, consider developing a federated learning model across smartphones in several countries; each region's data (text inputs) will have different linguistic and cultural characteristics.

As a result of this heterogeneity, model training presents unique challenges. The models must be robust enough to learn from diverse data distributions without overfitting to specific patterns that may exist in one client's dataset but not another's. This requires advanced aggregation algorithms that can effectively combine insights from vastly different data sources to create a universally applicable or highly adaptable model. This aspect of FL complicates the training process but also improves it by encouraging the development of models that are more inclusive and general.

1.3.3 General Workflow

The general workflow of Federated learning can be summarized in the following steps [2, 6]:

1. **Initialization:** The central server initializes a global model and distributes it to selected clients.
2. **Local Training:** Clients train the model on their local data and compute model updates (e.g., gradients).
3. **Model Update Sharing:** Clients send their model updates to the central server while keeping their raw data local.
4. **Aggregation:** The central server aggregates these updates (e.g., by averaging) to improve the global model.
5. **Model Broadcasting:** The updated global model is sent back to the clients for further training rounds.
6. **Iteration:** Steps 2–5 are repeated until the model achieves satisfactory performance.

The key components of federated learning include:

1. **Clients**: These are the nodes that have local data and participate in the learning process. They can be devices like smartphones, computers, or servers in different geographical locations.
2. **Central Server**: This is the entity that coordinates the learning process among clients. It aggregates the model updates from clients and sends the updated global model back to them.
3. **Local Models**: These are the machine learning models trained by each client on their local data.
4. **Global Model**: This is the aggregated model that is formed by the central server using the local models from the clients.

Table 1.2 illustrates the role of each entity in the federated learning process.

In the forthcoming second chapter, our journey will cover these subjects in greater depth and detail. The next chapter will provide a more comprehensive understanding of the details and complexities that define these topics.

Table 1.2 The role of entities in the federated learning process

Entity	Role in federated learning
Central Server	Coordinates the process, aggregates model updates, and updates the global model.
Client	Trains the model locally on its data and sends model updates to the central server.
Global Model	The model is being iteratively updated and improved through the FL process.
Local Data	Data that resides on the client's device and is used for local model training.

1.4   Brief History and Development

2016: The Birth of Federated Learning Google researchers introduced the term "Federated Learning" in a groundbreaking paper, presenting it as a way to train machine learning models across many devices while keeping all the training data local. This was a pivotal moment for machine learning, emphasizing privacy and data security by design [7].

2017–2018: Development of Federated Learning Frameworks As a result of federated learning's introduction, a variety of frameworks and algorithms have been developed to address the challenges it presents, including communication efficiency, data heterogeneity, and model aggregation. Federated Averaging (FedAvg) algorithms were developed during this period, which further enhanced the efficiency of model training across distributed networks [7].

2019: Becoming Famous The concept of federated learning started to gain recognition in the machine learning community. This was a significant shift from traditional centralized learning methods, as federated learning allowed organizations to train AI models on decentralized data without having to centralize or share that data [8]. This was particularly beneficial for preserving data privacy and reducing data transmission costs.

2020: Age of Integration Federated learning began to integrate with other learning frameworks, and various learning algorithms were explored to improve the basic federated averaging algorithm. This year marked the beginning of extensive research into optimizing federated learning algorithms to enhance their performance and efficiency [9].

2021: Merging with Other Methods The focus of research in federated learning shifted towards model fusion methods. These methods, including adaptive aggregation, regularization, clustered methods, and Bayesian methods, aimed to improve the way models trained on different devices were combined. This was a crucial step towards making federated learning more effective and practical [8, 9].

2022: Expanding to Other ML Areas The intersection of federated learning with other learning paradigms started to be discussed, termed federated X learning. Here, X includes multitask learning, meta-learning, transfer learning, unsupervised learning, and reinforcement learning. This represented a significant expansion of the scope of federated learning, opening up new possibilities for its application [9].

2023: Pushing Boundaries The emerging trends in federated learning continued to evolve, with a focus on addressing key challenges such as privacy, communication cost for model uploading and downloading, and statistical heterogeneity. This year saw significant advancements in the development of solutions to these challenges, making federated learning more robust and reliable [8, 9].

2024-Present: Seeking New Horizons Federated learning is now a well-established field with numerous applications. It continues to evolve, with ongoing research into improving efficiency, security, and the ability to handle non-IID (independent and identically distributed) data. The focus is on making federated learning more accessible and beneficial for a wide range of applications.

Figure 1.1 illustrates the mentioned milestones in the development of federated learning and its growing impact across various sectors. As federated learning continues to evolve, it is poised to play a crucial role in the future of privacy-preserving machine learning and cybersecurity.

1.5   The Role of Federated Learning in Cybersecurity

As a revolutionary innovation in cybersecurity, federated learning addresses critical issues such as data privacy, real-time threat detection, and collaborative defense mechanisms. FL ensures data privacy and security by enabling the training of machine learning models across decentralized datasets without transferring sensitive information. In cybersecurity, where the sharing of raw data can pose significant privacy concerns and compliance problems, this decentralized approach is particularly beneficial.

Among the primary advantages of FL in cybersecurity is its ability to facilitate real-time threat detection and response. FL allows individual entities, such as organizations or devices, to train models locally on their data and share model updates

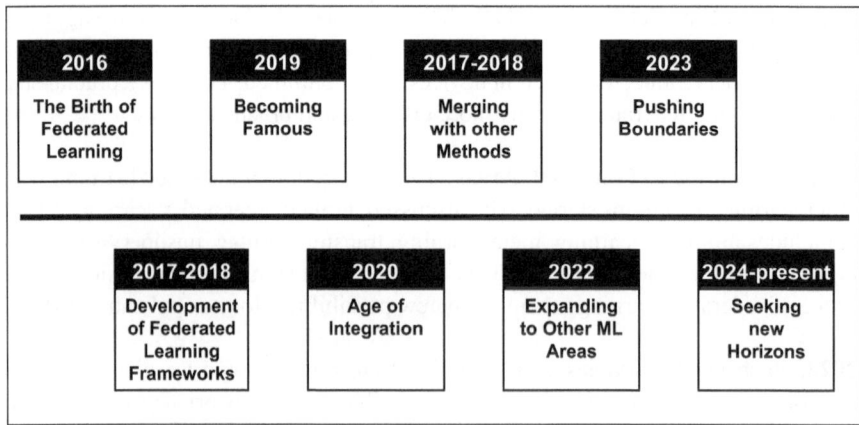

Fig. 1.1   A timeline of federated learning milestones

with a central server. This server aggregates updates and refines a global model, redistributed to all participants. This continuous and iterative process ensures that the global model is constantly updated with the latest threat intelligence. This enables faster and more effective detection of both emerging and evolving cyber threats.

For instance, FL's role in cybersecurity involves the healthcare sector, especially in protecting sensitive patient data. Cybercriminals increasingly target healthcare organizations due to their valuable personal and medical information. Sharing this data to improve cybersecurity measures is problematic with privacy concerns and regulatory challenges. Federated learning offers a solution by allowing healthcare providers to train machine learning models on their local datasets and share only model updates. For example, if a hospital identifies a ransomware attack, it can train its local model to recognize this threat. It can also send model updates to the federated server. The server aggregates these updates with those from other hospitals, producing a comprehensive global model redistributed to all participants. This collaborative model enables all healthcare providers to benefit from collective intelligence without compromising patient privacy. This enhances their ability to detect and respond to ransomware attacks more rapidly. In addition to enhancing threat detection and response, FL also plays a crucial role in developing a collaborative cybersecurity environment. Federated learning breaks down these barriers by enabling secure and privacy-preserving collaboration. This collective approach not only improves the accuracy and effectiveness of threat detection models but also creates a sense of shared responsibility and mutual benefit among participating entities. With federated learning, organizations can build more robust and adaptive cybersecurity defenses that can keep up with the rapidly evolving threat landscape by pooling their resources and expertise.

Consider the case of a large multinational corporation with offices located throughout the world. While each branch has valuable information on network activity, sharing this information centrally raises privacy concerns for employees and customers. FL allows these branches to train local models to detect phishing attempts, malware signatures, and other threats specific to their region. The central model then aggregates the knowledge collected from these local models, creating a comprehensive threat detection system that protects the entire organization without compromising user privacy.

As another example, FL can facilitate the development of robust anomaly detection systems. FL allows devices to learn the "normal" behavior of a network and flag any significant variations. This enables the detection of zero-day attacks, previously unknown threats before they cause widespread damage.

FL represents a significant advance in the fight against cyber threats. FL enables collaborative learning and anomaly detection while maintaining data privacy, enabling organizations to build robust and adaptive security systems. As the number of connected devices continues to increase, FL becomes an even more critical tool for protecting our digital future.

1.6 Summary

This chapter provides a comprehensive overview of federated learning, an innovative approach to machine learning that emphasizes data privacy and security. By enabling collaborative model training across decentralized data sources, FL addresses the limitations of traditional centralized learning models.

Centralized learning involves collecting data from multiple sources into a single server for processing, a practice that raises significant privacy and security risks. In contrast, FL emphasizes decentralized learning, allowing data to remain distributed and secure while being processed locally on individual devices.

The chapter explores the fundamental Definitions, Preliminaries, and General Concepts of Federated Learning, describing FL as a decentralized framework where multiple nodes collaboratively train a shared model while maintaining local data privacy. Each node computes model updates using its local data, and a central server aggregates these updates to refine the global model. This approach ensures the protection of sensitive information and underscores FL's unique workflow and principles.

The Brief History and Development of Federated Learning highlights its evolution, tracing key milestones and advancements from its inception to its application across diverse industries. This historical perspective showcases FL's transformative potential in reshaping machine learning practices and advancing its adoption for real-world challenges.

Finally, the chapter examines The Role of Federated Learning in Cybersecurity, focusing on how FL enhances data protection and reduces the risk of breaches and cyberattacks. By keeping data localized and ensuring secure model updates, FL emerges as a vital tool for safeguarding sensitive information across sectors such as healthcare, finance, and beyond. Through these discussions, the chapter establishes FL as a pivotal development in addressing modern machine learning's privacy and security challenges.

1.7 Conclusion

Federated learning provides robust solutions to the challenges posed by traditional centralized learning methods in machine learning. FL enhances data privacy and security by decentralizing the learning process. Additionally, this approach aligns with regulatory demands for data protection, which are increasing due to cyberattacks and data breaches. As centralized learning evolves to decentralized learning, data handling methodologies become more secure and efficient. FL provides a significant advancement in AI, maintaining data integrity while still benefiting from collective insights. With machine learning and cybersecurity continuing to develop, federated learning is poised to play a critical role. Thus, FL represents a pivotal step toward a more secure, efficient, and privacy-preserving approach to machine learning.

References

1. Yang, Q., Liu, Y., Chen, T., & Tong, Y. (2019). Federated machine learning. *ACM Transactions on Intelligent Systems and Technology, 10*, 1–19. https://doi.org/10.1145/3298981
2. Liu, J., Huang, J., Zhou, Y., et al. (2022). From distributed machine learning to federated learning: A survey. *Knowledge and Information Systems, 64*, 885–917. https://doi.org/10.1007/s10115-022-01664-x
3. Vergne, J. (2020). Decentralized vs. distributed organization: Blockchain, machine learning and the future of the digital platform. *Organ Theory, 1*, 263178772097705. https://doi.org/10.1177/2631787720977052
4. Verbraeken, J., Wolting, M., Katzy, J., et al. (2020). A survey on distributed machine learning. *ACM Computing Surveys, 53*, 1–33. https://doi.org/10.1145/3377454
5. Liu, B., Lv, N., Guo, Y., & Li, Y. (2024). Recent advances on federated learning: A systematic survey. *Neurocomputing, 597*, 128019. https://doi.org/10.1016/j.neucom.2024.128019
6. Yu, B., Mao, W., Lv, Y., et al. (2021). A survey on federated learning in data mining. *WIREs Data Mining and Knowledge Discovery, 12*. https://doi.org/10.1002/widm.1443
7. Li, L., Fan, Y., Tse, M., & Lin, K.-Y. (2020). A review of applications in federated learning. *Computers and Industrial Engineering, 149*, 106854. https://doi.org/10.1016/j.cie.2020.106854
8. Ji, S., Tan, Y., Saravirta, T., et al. (2024). Emerging trends in federated learning: From model fusion to federated X learning. *International Journal of Machine Learning and Cybernetics*. https://doi.org/10.1007/s13042-024-02119-1
9. Zhang, C., Xie, Y., Bai, H., et al. (2021). A survey on federated learning. *Knowledge-Based Systems, 216*, 106775. https://doi.org/10.1016/j.knosys.2021.106775

Chapter 2
Core Concepts of Federated Learning

2.1 Introduction

The concept of federated learning (FL) challenges the traditional paradigm of model training based on centralized data. A federated learning system, which distributes the computation process across many devices or "clients," is a distinct alternative to conventional methods where data is aggregated and processed on a central server. FL significance stems from its capability to learn from a diverse array of data points while preserving the data providers' privacy. Data intelligence has undergone a significant transition with the development of federated learning from centralized to decentralized machine learning. In the early stages of machine learning, most prediction models relied heavily on central datasets, which were often stored in a single location. As a result of this centralization, there are several challenges, such as high vulnerabilities to data breaches, as well as logistical difficulties surrounding data collection and storage. To address these issues, federated learning emerged as a decentralized model that enables learning to take place directly at the source of data. When we take a deeper look at the fundamental concepts of federated learning, it is crucial to understand not just the federated learning principles, but also the broader considerations associated with the use of federated learning as a technology [1].

2.2 Federated Learning Key Components, and Workflow

This section will provide a detailed description of the key components and workflow involved in Federated Learning. This section explores the fundamental elements of Federated Learning to offer a comprehensive understanding of how it works to ensure providing a robust and cohesive framework for the development of decentralized machine learning applications.

© The Author(s), under exclusive license to Springer Nature
Switzerland AG 2025
H. Tabrizchi, A. Aghasi, *Federated Cyber Intelligence*, SpringerBriefs in
Computer Science, https://doi.org/10.1007/978-3-031-86592-3_2

2.2.1 Key Components of Federated Learning Systems

Federated learning allows for the training of machine learning models while maintaining data privacy. It enables this by distributing the training process across a network of devices, or clients, that collaboratively learn from local datasets without sharing the data themselves. This section provides a description of the key components of a federated learning system.

2.2.1.1 Clients

Clients are the backbone of a federated learning system, comprising a variety of devices or entities that possess relevant data and computational resources. Client definition and roles are outlined below. Clients are defined as devices or entities participating in federated learning. They train a local model on their private data and contribute updates to a global model. Their role in federated learning involves three key aspects. As data providers, clients contribute their local datasets relevant to the learning task. These datasets can vary significantly across clients, leading to data heterogeneity. As local model trainers, clients utilize their local compute resources to train a copy of the global model on their data. Finally, as update contributors, clients send model updates, rather than raw data, to a central server for aggregation [1, 2].

Federated learning is driven by clients, which are individual nodes such as mobile phones, IoT devices, or even entire organizations like hospitals that generate their own data. As a result of this local computing, all sensitive data remains within the premises of the client, and only updates to the model are shared with the server. An example of this would be a predictive text model being developed across thousands of smartphones. As a client, each device learns from user inputs to predict text without ever sharing those inputs with a central server. As another example, hospitals could collaborate to improve diagnostic models without exchanging patient records [2]. The client roles in federated learning are shown in Table 2.1.

2.2.1.2 Server

The server acts as the central coordinator in a federated learning system, playing a pivotal role in model aggregation. This is to ensure collaborative learning progresses effectively. Both servers' definition and roles are outlined below. The server is

Table 2.1 Client roles in federated learning

Role	Description
Data holder/providers	Maintains possession of local data, ensuring privacy.
Local model trainer	Performs computations to update the local model slice.
Collaborator/update contributors	Participates in a collective effort to improve a global model.

defined as the central coordinator that facilitates learning across multiple distributed clients. Its most critical functions include model initialization, client selection, update collection, model aggregation, and model dissemination. Each of these functions contributes significantly to federated learning. Model initialization is the server's responsibility to create a global model that serves as the starting point for all clients. Client selection involves employing a strategy to choose participants for each training round. For update collection, the server receives model updates from participating clients. These updates are integral to the next stage. In model aggregation, the server combines the received updates to create a new, improved global model. In most federated learning systems, aggregation is typically performed by the server but can sometimes be delegated to a dedicated aggregator component. This process ensures effective learning while maintaining data privacy and system integrity across diverse and distributed datasets. Finally, model dissemination involves the server sending the updated global model back to the clients following aggregation. This ensures all participants have the latest version for further training rounds [2, 3].

The server in a federated learning setup coordinates the learning process by sending the global model to selected clients, receives the locally updated models from clients, and aggregates these updates to improve the global model. The server's most crucial role is aggregating the model updates it receives from clients. This process must ensure that the aggregated model performs well on unseen data, maintaining accuracy and generalizability [3]. Table 2.2 outlines the critical roles the server plays throughout the federated learning process, from initializing the model to distributing updated versions post-aggregation.

2.2.1.3   Aggregator

The aggregator, often part of the server, uses algorithms like Federated Averaging (FedAvg) to combine updates received from clients. This involves calculating a weighted average of the updates, where weights often correspond to the volume of

Table 2.2 Client roles in federated learning

Role	Description
Model initialization	The server initializes a global model, which serves as the starting point for all clients.
Client selection	The server employs a client selection strategy to choose participants for each training round.
Update collection	The server receives model updates from participating clients.
Model aggregation	The server aggregates the received updates to create a new, improved global model.
Model dissemination	Following aggregation, the server sends the updated global model back to the clients for further training rounds, ensuring all participants have the latest version.

data each client possesses. The effectiveness of the aggregation algorithm directly impacts the final model's performance and the privacy guarantees it offers [1, 3]. In a federated learning system, an aggregator is typically part of a server, but there are alternative designs:

1. **Distributed Aggregator Nodes**: In some advanced or more decentralized federated learning setups, the aggregation process can be handled by dedicated aggregator nodes. These nodes are separate from the central server and can be strategically placed within the network. This setup can help reduce the load on a single server and increase the resilience and scalability of the system.
2. **Edge Servers**: In edge computing environments, aggregation can be performed by edge servers, which are located closer to where the data is generated. This not only helps in reducing latency and bandwidth usage but also distributes the computational load more evenly across the network.
3. **Client Devices**: In highly decentralized models, aggregation can also occur directly on client devices. Here, a subset of clients or all clients collaboratively perform the aggregation tasks themselves, possibly rotating the role of aggregator among them to balance load and minimize points of failure.
4. **Hybrid Models**: Some systems may use a hybrid approach where initial aggregation is done in smaller groups or clusters (such as at the edge level), and further aggregation of these preliminary results is performed at a central server or a dedicated aggregator node.

These four alternatives each have their own trade-offs in regard to efficiency, privacy, scalability, and fault tolerance, and the choice depends on the specifics of the federated learning application. An aggregator designed well can mitigate the problems associated with heterogeneous data and skewed client participation in Sects. 2.4.1.1 and 2.4.1.2, respectively.

2.2.1.4   Client Selector or Client Coordinator

In a federated learning system, the client selector, typically part of the central coordination mechanism housed on the server, is responsible for selecting which clients participate in each training round. The client selector ensures that the criteria for participation are met and that the selection process supports the objectives of the federated learning model, such as diversity, fairness, and efficiency. Effective client selection strategies consider several key factors.

Clients with sufficient computational power and battery life are prioritized to ensure resource availability. This ensures that selected clients can complete their tasks without disruptions. Clients whose data is representative or valuable for the current learning task are chosen based on data relevance. To optimize communication efficiency, clients capable of maintaining a stable connection to the server are selected [3]. Clients with diverse data are often chosen to ensure the model learns generalizable features, addressing data diversity. To maintain fairness, strategies may involve rotating clients to avoid biases toward data from frequently selected participants. These considerations collectively enhance model performance and efficiency in federated learning systems.

2.2.2 General Workflow of Federated Learning Systems

In federated learning systems, machine learning models are built through an iterative process under the constraints of data privacy and distributed ownership. It is crucial to understand how individual components of a federated learning system work together to achieve the goal of collaborative, decentralized learning without compromising data security. In the previous section, the key components of a FL system were discussed [3–5]. The purpose of this section is to explore the architecture and workflow of a general FL system, to see how these components are coordinated and how they work together to produce an effective and cohesive learning process.

2.2.2.1 Initialization

The federated learning process begins with the **Client Coordinator**, previously named the entity responsible for client management, initializing the global model. This model serves as the starting point for all computations. By setting initial parameters and distributing this model to selected clients, the server ensures that each participant has the same starting point.

2.2.2.2 Client Selection

In this stage, the Client Coordinator selects a subset of clients to participate in the current training session. This selection can be based on various criteria such as availability, data relevance, data diversity, and historical participation. It aims to optimize the learning process and manage network resources effectively. The selection strategy can vary greatly depending on the specific requirements of the federated learning application, such as prioritizing data privacy, minimizing communication overhead, or enhancing model accuracy.

2.2.2.3 Local Model Training

Once selected, each client trains the model locally using their own data. This means that the raw data never leaves the client's device, maintaining privacy. Each client uses the global model parameters as a base and updates these parameters based on insights gained from their local data. Depending on the client's computational capabilities and data characteristics, the training process can be customized.

2.2.2.4 Model Updates Collection

After local training, clients send their model updates—typically gradients or parameter changes, not the raw data—to the server. This step is crucial as it involves secure communication channels to prevent data leakage and ensure that the transmitted information remains confidential.

2.2.2.5 Aggregation

The server, through its aggregator component, then combines all received updates to produce a new global model. This aggregation can employ various algorithms, such as Federated Averaging (FedAvg), which typically computes a weighted average of the updates. The weights can be based on the quantity or quality of data each client contributes, thereby addressing issues like data heterogeneity and skewed client participation.

2.2.2.6 Model Evaluation and Adjustment

The updated global model is then evaluated to assess its performance. Evaluation can be done using a separate validation dataset maintained by the server or through performance feedback received from clients. As a result of the evaluation results, the server may adjust learning rates, alter client selection strategies, or update aggregation algorithms to improve future rounds.

2.2.2.7 Model Dissemination

All participating clients are sent the newly aggregated global model for further training. As a result of this dissemination, not only is each client working with the most current model version, but also the performance of the model can be quickly converged across different data distributions and client environments.

2.2.2.8 Iteration

Multiple rounds of the process are conducted from client selection to dissemination of the model until it meets the predetermined stopping criteria or achieves satisfactory performance. Throughout each iteration, the model is refined further, incorporating a broader range of insights from the distributed dataset.

2.2.2.9   Deployment

The model can be deployed either as a standalone application or integrated into existing systems where it can make predictions or facilitate decision-making once it has been sufficiently trained and meets all performance, privacy, and security standards.

The general workflow highlights the complex, multi-step nature of federated learning, emphasizing the balance between local autonomy and centralized coordination. Each stage is designed to make use of distributed data sources effectively while maintaining stringent privacy and security standards. Figure 2.1 provides an illustration of the flowchart of the federated learning workflow, detailing each key step from initialization to the deployment of these systems.

2.2.3   Federated Learning Algorithms

In the previous sections, we explored the components, structure, and interactions within federated learning systems. This section shifts focus to the core algorithms that underpin federated learning. The foundational algorithm, Federated Averaging (FedAvg), introduced by McMahan et al. [6], represents the starting point of federated learning. Building upon this foundation, subsequent algorithms such as FedSGD and FedProx have been developed to improve FedAvg's performance, particularly in challenging scenarios involving non-independent and identically distributed (non-IID) data and non-ideal client conditions [7].

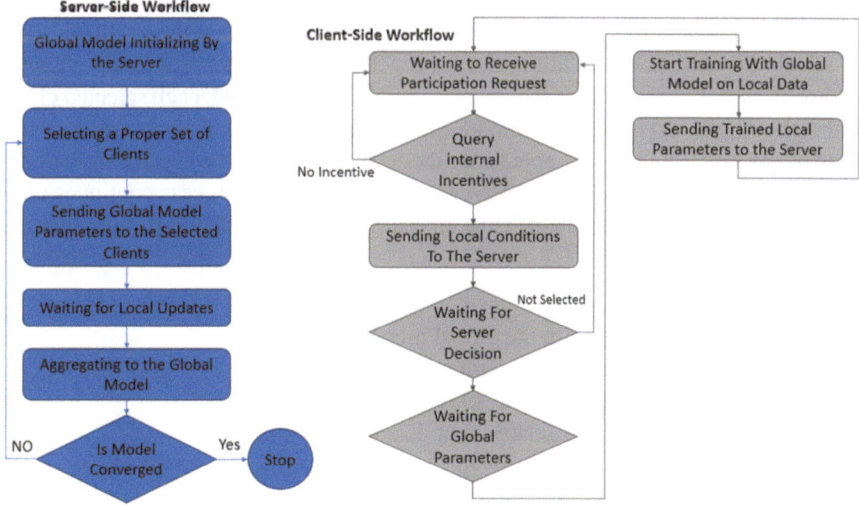

Fig. 2.1 General workflow of an FL system

McMahan et al. pioneered the concept of federated learning, a decentralized approach to machine learning. The central algorithm, FedAvg, operates by aggregating the weights of locally trained models to construct a global model. This global model is then distributed back to local clients for further training. The pseudocode for the FedAvg algorithm is provided below:

Algorithm 2.1 FedAVG

Input: Global model weights
Output: Updated local weights

1. Initialize global model weights W_global
2. **For** each round *t* do:
3.   Select random set of K clients from all clients
4.   Initialize an empty set of client model weights: W_clients = []
5.   **For** each client *k* in a random subset of clients do:
6.   Initialize local model weights: W_local = W_global
7.   **For** each local epoch *i* from 1 to E do:
8.   **For** each minibatch *B* in client's local dataset do:
9.   W_local = LocalUpdate(B, W_local)
10.   Append local model weights to client model weights
11. W_global = average(W_clients)

In this pseudocode:

- W_global represents the global model weights.
- W_clients is a set of model weights from each client.
- W_local represents the local model weights for each client.
- LocalUpdate(B,W_local) is a function that updates W_local based on the mini batch B.
- average(W_clients) is a function that computes the average of W_clients.

At the beginning of the federated learning process, the server selects a random set of clients to participate and initializes them with a fresh model. Subsequently, several rounds of updates and averaging commence. In each round, each selected client trains the newly received global model using its local data. This local training consists of the same numbers of epochs until convergence. The locally updated model weights are then sent back to the server for averaging. This process continues until the server decides to terminate it. Thus, in each round *t*, the following operations are performed:

1. Select random clients.
2. Initialize local models with the global model.
3. Train local models on local data for several epochs.
4. Send local model updates to the server.
5. Average the local model updates to update the global model.

Following equations describes the local training and global aggregating procedures in FedAVG

$$w_{t+1}^k \leftarrow \textit{client Update Model}\left(k, w_t\right) \qquad (2.1)$$

$$w_{t+1} = \sum_{k=1}^{K} \frac{n_k}{n} w_{t+1}^k \qquad (2.2)$$

Equation (2.1) points out the local training phase where each client k using global model aggregated at round t performs training to reach the converged model w_{t+1}^k.

The aggregation phase, Eq. (2.2), contains a weighted average over all received local models. $\frac{n_k}{n}$ actually indicates how much data in comparison to all data resides in client k. It is completely expected that the weight of clients with more data must be more in the global model. An overview of the FedAVG is illustrated in Fig. 2.2.

The performance of the aggregated model in FedAvg could be improved if the model parameters of the clients were aggregated after each local epoch instead of waiting until all training epochs are completed. This is the core idea behind the FedSGD algorithm, introduced in the same paper following FedAvg. In FedSGD, after each local epoch, the clients send their gradients to the server. Unlike in FedAvg, where simple averaging is performed, FedSGD aggregates the gradients and optimizes the loss function using these local gradients (g_k). The gradient descent formula, Eq. (2.3), is applied on the server, making the aggregation more efficient and potentially enhancing model performance.

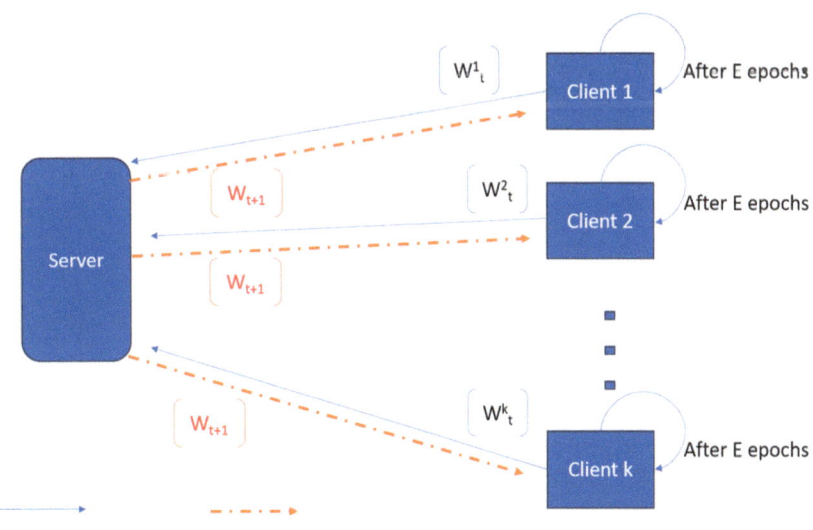

Local model update   Global model update

Fig. 2.2 FedAvg operation scheme

$$w_{t+1} = w_t - \gamma \sum_{k=1}^{K} \frac{n_k}{n} g_k \tag{2.3}$$

The primary difference in FedSGD is the use of a weighted average of all collected gradients. After performing backward propagation, each client sends its calculated gradient to the server, which then updates the global model weights. The updated weights are subsequently broadcasted back to the clients to start the next epoch. It is evident that this approach incurs a significantly higher communication cost compared to the FedAvg algorithm.

The transition from FedAVG to FedSGD can be rationalized by considering the trade-off between communication efficiency and model performance. While FedAVG reduces the communication cost, it might have poorer performance due to the naive method of averaging the model weight. Therefore, if the communication cost is not a concern and the focus is on improving the model performance, transitioning to FedSGD could be a rational choice.

In the real world, clients often face issues such as poor connectivity, power shortages, or CPU overutilization, leading to incomplete training epochs. In FedAvg, stragglers are simply dropped, degrading model performance due to the loss of valuable data. To address this heterogeneity,

Tian Li et al. proposed the FedProx algorithm in [8]. FedProx accommodates varying numbers of epochs, allowing some devices to perform fewer epochs based on current system constraints.

Figure 2.3 illustrates a set of clients selected for participation. A subset of these clients completes their training epochs (active set), while others become stragglers. FedProx permits stragglers to upload their partially trained models.

While FedAvg assumes that data are independent and identically distributed and guarantees convergence under this assumption, this is often unrealistic. FedProx generalizes FedAvg to handle non-IID data. The global model weights are superior to any individual client model because the server aggregates more data. Therefore, if a client's model parameters approach the global model parameters, it indicates the

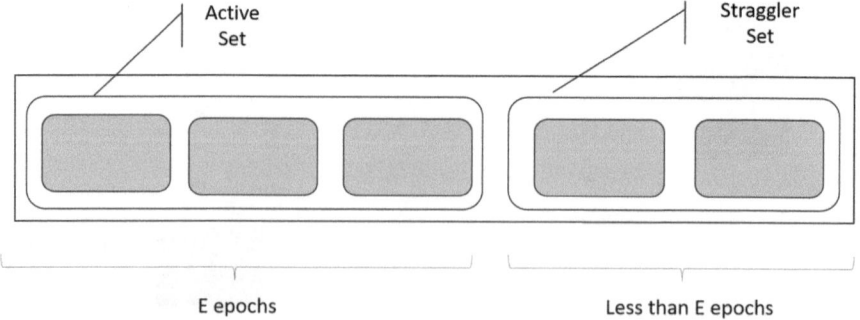

Fig. 2.3 FedProx client partitioning

client is on the right path. FedProx incorporates a proximal term into the client's learning equation to control the update, ensuring convergence.

$$w_{t+1} = w_t - \gamma \left(g + \mu \left(w_t - w_G \right) \right) \tag{2.4}$$

The proximal term, $\mu(w_t - w_G)$, guides the local model by considering the global model direction, facilitating convergence even with non-IID data.

FedProx addresses the issues of client heterogeneity and non-IID data by allowing flexible training epochs and incorporating a proximal term that regulates local updates. This makes FedProx a more robust and adaptable algorithm for federated learning in real-world scenarios, where client capabilities and data distributions are often diverse and unpredictable.

FedAvg [6], FedSGD [8], and FedProx [9] represent foundational and evolving approaches to federated learning, each addressing specific challenges inherent in decentralized machine learning. FedAvg introduced the basic concept of federated learning by averaging locally trained model weights, setting the stage for more sophisticated algorithms. FedSGD built upon this by aggregating gradients after each local epoch, optimizing the global model more frequently but at a higher communication cost. FedProx further advanced the field by accommodating client heterogeneity and handling non-IID data through a proximal term that guides local updates to align with the global model. Together, these algorithms form the backbone of federated learning systems, each contributing unique solutions to enhance performance, robustness, and scalability in real-world applications. As federated learning continues to evolve, these foundational algorithms will undoubtedly inspire future innovations and adaptations to meet emerging challenges and opportunities.

2.2.3.1 Difference of Federated Learning's Workflow and Architecture

There are distinct aspects to the federated learning's workflow and architecture which relate to its design and function. The architecture of federated learning describes the structural design of the system. This includes the arrangement and relationships of its core components such as clients, a central server, an aggregator, communication networks, and security mechanisms. It defines how these components are organized and interact to facilitate the overall system's operation. In contrast, as mentioned in the previous section, the workflow of federated learning refers to the sequence of processes and activities carried out within this architectural framework. It details the step-by-step procedures involved in training and updating the machine learning model, from the initial model distribution by the central server to the clients, through local training on clients' devices, to the aggregation of updates and the iterative refinement of the model. In a nutshell, while the architecture provides the blueprint for the system's infrastructure, the workflow describes the dynamic operations and tasks executed within that infrastructure to achieve federated learning objectives [10].

2.2.3.2   General Architectures of Federated Learning Systems

Within the domain of federated learning, there are several architectures, primarily categorized into horizontal federated learning, vertical federated learning, hybrid federated learning and federated transfer learning. These categorizations are based on the nature of the data partitioning and the type of learning involved [9].

2.2.3.2.1   Horizontal Federated Learning (HFL)

Horizontal federated learning, also known as sample-based federated learning, applies to scenarios where datasets from different clients share the same feature space but differ in samples. In horizontal federated learning, each participating client has a dataset with the same features but different records. The main goal is to collaboratively train a global model without sharing the local data. This approach is beneficial when each client has a large number of unique samples. The workflow and algorithms explained so far are applicable with no change for horizontal FL.

2.2.3.2.2   Vertical Federated Learning (VFL)

In vertical federated learning, each client has datasets containing different features but with the same sample IDs. The focus is on learning a combined model that utilizes all features from different datasets without sharing the raw data. The workflow and algorithms is provided below:

1. **Initialization**: A global model is initialized.
2. **Feature Alignment**: Match the sample IDs across clients to align features.
3. **Local Computation**: Clients compute intermediate results based on their local features and send these to a central server or a coordinating client.
4. **Model Aggregation**: The server or coordinating client combines the intermediate results to update the model. FedSGD is a good candidate for vertical FL aggregation
5. **Update Global Model**: The model parameters are updated and shared back with clients.
6. **Iteration**: Steps 3–5 are repeated until the model converges.

In a nutshell, the applications of Vertical Federated Learning include scenarios such as financial institutions where banks and insurance companies collaborate to build a credit scoring model using different types of data they possess about the same individuals, and cross-silo learning scenarios where different companies collaborate to enhance a model without revealing their proprietary data. In Vertical Federated Learning, the server's role in aggregation involves combining intermediate results from different clients to update the global model. This process is more complex than in Horizontal Federated Learning due to the need to handle different features across the clients while maintaining the integrity of the sample alignment. Here's a detailed explanation of how the server performs aggregation in Vertical Federated Learning:

Feature alignment in Vertical Federated Learning involves two key aspects. Sample matching ensures that the samples across clients are aligned, with each sample uniquely identified, often through a common identifier such as a user ID. Feature distribution ensures that each client has a unique subset of features while sharing the same samples with other clients. In the local computation phase, clients compute partial gradients or intermediate values using their local features and the current model parameters. To maintain privacy, these computations are often performed using secure multiparty computation (MPC) techniques or homomorphic encryption to prevent the exposure of raw data.

Intermediate results are then shared, where clients may encrypt their intermediate results before sending them to the server. These encrypted results are transmitted to the central server. At the server side, aggregation involves decryption (if needed), followed by combining the partial gradients or intermediate values from all clients. This step often includes summing the partial gradients or using weighted averaging, particularly if data distributions differ significantly. The combined gradients are then used to perform a step of gradient descent, updating the global model parameters.

Model updates occur when the server updates the global model parameters using the aggregated gradients and distributes the updated parameters back to the clients. This iterative process, comprising local computation, intermediate result sharing, and aggregation, continues until the global model converges. For example, in a collaborative scenario, a bank and an insurance company might build a predictive model by combining their unique features while ensuring data privacy and security.

Algorithm 2.2 Vertical Federated Learning Framework

Input: local datasets DBDB (Bank Client) and DIDI (Insurance Client), initial global model parameters W, learning rate η, maximum number of iterations T
Output: converged global model parameters W^*

1. Initialization: Each client (Bank BB and Insurance II) initializes its local dataset DBDB, DIDI, and accesses the shared sample alignment. The server initializes global model parameters W.
2. **For** each t from 1 to T do:
3. Local Computation: Each client computes its partial gradients using its local features and current global model parameters W: ∇WB = ComputeGradients(DB,W), ∇WI = ComputeGradients(DI,W)
4. Secure Sharing: Clients encrypt their computed gradients to maintain privacy: E(∇WB) = Encrypt(∇WB), E(∇WI) = Encrypt(∇WI), Encrypted gradients E(∇WB) and E(∇WI) are sent to the server.
5. Aggregation at the Server: The server decrypts the received gradients, if necessary: ∇WB = Decrypt(E(∇WB)), ∇WI = Decrypt(E(∇WI)); The server aggregates the gradients from all clients: ∇W = ∇WB + ∇WI
6. Global Model Update: The server updates the global model parameters using the aggregated gradients: $W \leftarrow W - \eta\nabla W$
7. Distribution of Updated Model: The updated global model parameters W are sent back to all clients.
8. Convergence Check: If the global model has converged, based on a predefined loss threshold or maximum iterations, stop.
9. **end for**

2.2.3.2.3   Federated Transfer Learning (FTL)

Federated transfer learning addresses situations where datasets across clients have different samples and different features. It uses transfer learning techniques to adapt knowledge from one domain to another. The workflow and algorithms is provided below:

1. **Initialization**: Initialize source and target models.
2. **Knowledge Transfer**: Use a pre-trained model on a related task (source domain) and adapt it to the target domain.
3. **Local Training**: Each client trains its part of the model on local data.
4. **Transfer Learning**: Apply transfer learning techniques to refine the model on the target data.
5. **Model Aggregation**: Aggregate updates from clients to refine the model iteratively.

FTL can be applied in various scenarios where a pretrained model can be shared. For instance, consider scenarios where one client has rich, labeled data, and others have unlabeled or less representative data, benefiting from the rich data's pre-trained models. And for a deeper understanding let's delve into a collaborative healthcare system. In this scenario, the participants include a source client, which is a large hospital possessing extensive labeled medical imaging data and a pre-trained diagnostic model, and a target client, a smaller clinic with fewer labeled data points and different features such as patient demographics and symptoms. The workflow begins with the hospital's robust diagnostic model, developed using a dataset with image-based features. The clinic, lacking sufficient data to train a high-performance model from scratch, has its own data, including demographics, symptoms, and a few labeled MRI scans. The hospital transfers its pre-trained model to the clinic, which fine-tunes it using its local data. The clinic adapts this model with its limited labeled MRI scans and additional features while the hospital continues to refine its model with its extensive dataset. Both entities share their updated model parameters securely with a central server to protect patient privacy. The central server aggregates these parameters, leveraging the hospital's extensive imaging data and the clinic's diverse feature set to create a generalized diagnostic model. The updated global model is then distributed back to both the hospital and the clinic. This process iterates, further refining the model through additional rounds of local adaptation and aggregation.

2.2.3.2.4   Hybrid Federated Learning (HFL)

Hybrid Federated Learning combines elements of both Horizontal Federated Learning and Vertical Federated Learning. This approach is designed to handle scenarios where datasets across different clients may have overlapping features and samples as well as distinct features and samples. Hybrid Federated Learning aims to use the strengths of both horizontal and vertical data partitions to build more comprehensive and robust models. This type of Federated Learning is particularly suited for scenarios where there is overlap in samples and features among clients, as they may have datasets with some shared features and samples alongside unique ones. It is also ideal for cross-domain collaboration, where organizations from different fields, such as healthcare and finance, work together to develop a model that leverages data from both domains while ensuring sensitive information remains secure and private.

The aggregation process in Hybrid Federated Learning involves several key steps. During the initial setup, each client has its own dataset, which may overlap with other clients in terms of samples and features, while a central server coordinates the training process and handles the aggregation of model updates. Clients begin by performing local computations on their datasets. For shared features, clients compute gradients or updates collaboratively, while for unique features, they perform computations tailored to their local data. Once computations are complete, clients generate intermediate results, such as gradients or weights, for both shared and unique features. These results are typically encrypted to maintain data privacy before being sent to the server. The server then aggregates updates for shared features across clients while handling unique feature updates separately, ensuring the global model benefits from all contributions without compromising privacy. Using the aggregated updates, the server updates the global model parameters and redistributes the updated model to all clients for further local training. This cycle of local computation, intermediate result sharing, and aggregation is repeated iteratively until the global model converges. To better understanding let's review an example scenario in detail.

Consider a scenario where a healthcare organization and a fitness app company collaborate to build a predictive model for health outcomes. The healthcare organization has medical records, while the fitness app company has activity data. Some individuals use both services, providing overlapping samples.

In a hybrid federated learning scenario, the process begins with an initial setup involving two clients and a server. Client 1, a healthcare organization, holds medical records such as blood pressure and cholesterol levels, while Client 2, a fitness app company, possesses activity data like steps and heart rate. The server manages the global model and coordinates the aggregation of updates. During local computation, both clients train their models locally. For shared features, corresponding to overlapping individuals, they compute gradients or updates. For unique features—such as medical records for Client 1 and activity data for Client 2—they perform specific updates tailored to their datasets. Following local computation, both clients encrypt their intermediate results to preserve privacy and send the encrypted results to the server. The server decrypts these results, if necessary, and aggregates the updates for shared features. It processes updates for unique features separately to ensure that all contributions enhance the global model while maintaining data privacy. The server then updates the global model parameters using the aggregated updates and sends the updated model back to the clients. This process iterates through multiple rounds of computation, sharing, and aggregation until the global model achieves convergence.

Federated learning enables collaborative model training while preserving data privacy across diverse scenarios through four main architectures. Horizontal Federated Learning addresses situations where clients have the same features but different samples, utilizing model updates aggregation by a central server. Vertical Federated Learning handles datasets with different features but the same samples by aligning features and combining partial gradients. Federated Transfer Learning applies transfer learning techniques to scenarios with different features and samples, transferring a pre-trained model from a source to a target client for local adaptation. Hybrid Federated Learning integrates both horizontal and vertical approaches to manage datasets with overlapping and unique features and samples, aggregating updates for both shared and unique data aspects. Each architecture ensures robust, secure, and privacy-preserving collaborative learning tailored to specific data distribution needs. For more detail read [10].

2.3   An Overview of Key Components of Federated Learning, Synchronization Strategies, and Coordination Mechanisms

This subsection explores federated learning's core components, including the interactions between clients, servers, and networks that enable collaborative machine learning while preserving data privacy and computational efficiency.

2.3.1   Key Components of Federated Learning

Through federated learning, multiple decentralized entities, or clients, can collaborate to train machine learning models, while keeping the data local. Unlike traditional Machine Learning systems, which rely on a centralized architecture where data is collected, preprocessed, and used to train models on a central server before validation and deployment, federated learning maintains data privacy and security by ensuring that raw data does not leave the client's location. This approach allows nodes in the distributed system to independently perform model training, using the strengths of centralized systems for data processing and model management. It capitalizes on distributed systems' scalability, fault tolerance, and performance enhancements. To enable distributed machine learning while preserving data privacy and ensuring efficient model training, federated learning uses a sophisticated system of interconnected components. In this system, the Clients are the foundational elements of this system, typically comprising edge devices like smartphones, IoT devices, or specialized systems such as hospital networks. These clients maintain their own local datasets and perform computational tasks independently, which contributes to the overall data diversity of the learning process. The Central Server orchestrates the entire federated learning ecosystem. It initializes the global model, coordinates client activities, distributes training tasks, and aggregates updates from various clients. This is done to refine and improve the model continuously. A robust communication network connects these clients and the central server, managing secure data transfers and ensuring reliable information exchange. This network must be capable of handling high-volume data transmissions and frequent communications. The aggregator, typically integrated into the central server, consolidates model updates from different clients. Using advanced algorithms like Federated Averaging, it addresses the challenges of data heterogeneity and manages variations in client participation. Security Mechanisms are embedded to protect sensitive information, employing techniques like secure multi-party computation and differential privacy. These mechanisms ensure data integrity and prevent unauthorized access during model aggregation. The Model Validation Module evaluates the performance of the aggregated model against predefined standards, utilizing centralized or distributed validation datasets to fine-tune and assess model effectiveness. Lastly, the Data Management Layer handles crucial logistical aspects such as metadata management, client availability tracking, and resource scheduling. This component ensures smooth coordination and efficient task distribution across the distributed network. As shown in Table 2.3, these components work together to enable collaborative machine learning while maintaining data privacy and security [11].

2.3.2   Synchronization Strategies for Federated Learning

As discussed throughout the chapter, the central idea of federated learning revolves around aggregating collected model updates. Synchronization strategies in federated learning refer to the various methods used to coordinate and integrate these local updates into the global model. Given the challenges of communication, computation, and privacy, synchronization strategies play a crucial role in determining the efficiency, performance, and privacy of the system. Depending on whether the clients synchronize in each round or not, these strategies are categorized into synchronous scenarios, asynchronous scenarios, hybrid strategies, and hierarchical synchronization [11, 12].

2.3.2.1   Centralized Synchronization

Centralized synchronization is a strategy where a central server manages model update coordination. This process operates in rounds: the server sends the current global model to a subset of clients, who train it with their local data. After training, the clients send their updates back to the server, which aggregates them, typically using Federated Averaging, to create a new global model. This cycle continues until a certain number of rounds are completed or a convergence condition is achieved. The main advantages of this approach are its simplicity, central control, and

Table 2.3 Components enabling collaborative machine learning

Key components	Description	Key functions
Clients	Typically edge devices or local servers that hold data relevant to the federated learning task, such as smartphones, IoT devices, or hospital systems. They perform computations locally and maintain their own datasets, contributing to data diversity.	Maintains own dataset Performs local computations
Central server	Acts as the orchestrator of the federated learning process, coordinating clients, distributing tasks, and aggregating updates. It sends the initial global model to clients and collects updates post-training to refine the global model.	Model initialization Client coordination Task distribution Aggregation of updates
Communication network	Connects clients with the central server, handling data transfers and ensuring secure communication. This network must be robust to manage high volumes of data and frequent communications.	Manages data transfers Ensures secure communication
Aggregator	Usually part of the central server, it aggregates model updates from clients using algorithms like Federated Averaging (FedAvg). This component is crucial for addressing data heterogeneity and skewed client participation.	Aggregates model updates Optimizes the global model
Security mechanisms	Equipped with advanced security features such as secure multi-party computation (SMPC) and differential privacy to protect client data during aggregation and ensure the integrity of the federated learning process.	Protects client data Ensures system integrity
Model validation module	Evaluates the performance of the aggregated model against predefined standards and objectives. It may utilize validation datasets that are centrally held or distributed across clients participating in validation rounds.	Evaluates model performance Fine-tunes the model
Data management layer	Handles metadata, client availability, data distributions, and other logistical aspects of the federated learning system. This component supports the smooth and efficient management of resources and scheduling of tasks across the distributed network.	Manages metadata and logistics Supports resource and task scheduling

predictable communication patterns. However, it also has drawbacks, such as scalability limitations, potential communication bottlenecks, and a single point of failure.

2.3.2.2 Asynchronous Synchronization

Asynchronous synchronization allows clients to send updates to a central server independently, without waiting for other clients or the completion of a global round. This strategy features flexible communication, as clients can upload their updates whenever they are ready. The server integrates them into the global model upon receipt. This reduces idle time, allowing users to work at their own pace. Asynchronous synchronization offers greater flexibility, reduced synchronization delays, and improved scalability. However, it also has potential downsides, such as model inconsistency and the need for more complex aggregation techniques to manage asynchronous updates. It is even possible to have multiple zones of synchrony where separate aggregators control client synchronization. This approach is known as hierarchical synchronization.

2.3.2.3 Hierarchical Synchronization

Hierarchical synchronization in federated learning involves a multi-tiered coordination system. This strategy typically divides clients into groups or regions, with each group having its own aggregator. These groups perform local aggregation before sending results to a central server for further processing. This approach reduces communication overhead, improving scalability and allowing localized learning. However, hierarchical synchronization has its challenges, including increased complexity and the need for careful design to maintain consistency across different groups.

2.3.2.4 Hybrid Synchronization

Hybrid synchronization strategies aim to balance the benefits of both synchronous and asynchronous modes. In this approach, clients are divided into groups based on their computational power, network latency, or other factors. High-capacity clients might operate synchronously within their group, while lower-capacity clients work asynchronously. This strategy can improve resource utilization while maintaining a reasonable level of global consistency. However, hybrid models introduce complexities in aggregation and coordination that need to be managed, particularly when reconciling updates from asynchronous clients with synchronous rounds.

2.3.2.5 Adaptive Synchronization

Adaptive synchronization dynamically adjusts the coordination strategy based on system conditions such as network bandwidth, client availability, or computational load. For example, during periods of high network congestion, the system may switch from synchronous to asynchronous updates. Conversely, if client updates are highly inconsistent, the system can enforce synchronization to align model parameters more closely. This dynamic adaptability enhances the resilience of federated learning systems, particularly in heterogeneous and volatile environments, making it well-suited for real-world deployments.

2.3.2.6 Security and Robustness in Synchronization

Synchronization strategies also play a critical role in ensuring federated learning security and robustness. For instance, asynchronous updates can introduce vulnerabilities, such as model poisoning attacks, where delayed or malicious updates corrupt the global model. Strategies like robust aggregation algorithms, Byzantine fault tolerance, or differential privacy can mitigate these risks. Furthermore, hierarchical synchronization can help localize the impact of such attacks to smaller groups, reducing widespread disruption.

2.3.2.7 Edge-Based Synchronization

Edge-based synchronization leverages edge servers as intermediate aggregators between clients and the central server. These edge servers collect updates from nearby clients, perform localized aggregation, and send the results to the central server. This approach reduces communication latency, alleviates server-side bottlenecks, and is particularly effective in applications like IoT systems and smart cities. However, ensuring consistency across different edge servers requires robust mechanisms, especially when dealing with updates from resource-constrained clients.

Table 2.4 summarizes the key synchronization strategies discussed in this section, highlighting their defining features, advantages, and challenges.

2.4 Federated Learning Challenges and Solutions

This section explores the critical challenges in federated learning and presents strategies to address them effectively.

2.4.1 Challenges

This section examines some of the most critical challenges facing federated learning [13].

2.4.1.1 Data Heterogeneity

Data heterogeneity in federated learning refers to the scenario where data across different clients vary widely in terms of volume, distribution, and underlying characteristics. This variability can lead to a model that performs well on data from some clients but poorly on others.

Table 2.4 Summarization of synchronization strategies

Synchronization strategy	Description	Advantages	Challenges
Centralized synchronization	A central server coordinates model updates in rounds.	Simplicity, central control, predictable communication patterns.	Scalability limitations, communication bottlenecks, single point of failure.
Asynchronous synchronization	Clients independently send updates to the server without waiting for others.	Greater flexibility, reduced synchronization delays, improved scalability.	Model inconsistency, complex aggregation techniques needed for asynchronous updates.
Hierarchical synchronization	Multi-tiered system where groups of clients perform local aggregation before sending results to a central server.	Reduces communication overhead, improves scalability, allows localized learning.	Increased complexity, requires careful consistency design across groups.
Hybrid synchronization	Combines synchronous and asynchronous strategies for different client groups based on their characteristics.	Balances resource utilization, maintains global consistency.	Complex coordination and aggregation, reconciliation challenges.
Adaptive synchronization	Dynamically adjusts synchronization strategy based on system conditions.	Enhances resilience in heterogeneous environments, flexible for real-world use.	Requires dynamic monitoring and strategy adjustment mechanisms.
Security and robustness	Incorporates mechanisms like robust aggregation and differential privacy to ensure security.	Mitigates risks like poisoning attacks, reduces disruption scope.	Additional computational and algorithmic complexity.
Edge-based synchronization	Uses edge servers as intermediate aggregators to collect updates and reduce central server load.	Lowers latency, alleviates bottlenecks, effective in IoT and smart cities.	Consistency issues across edge servers, challenges with resource-constrained clients.

2.4.1.2 Skewed Client Participation

Skewed client participation occurs when certain clients are more frequently selected or able to participate in the training rounds than others, which can bias the model towards the data characteristics of these clients.

2.4.1.3 Communication Challenges in Federated Learning

While federated learning has been successful in alleviating the strain on communication infrastructure by bringing the code to the data, it is not without its challenges. One of the primary issues arises from the increasing number of end users attempting to update the central server, which can create bottlenecks, particularly when the clients have significantly weaker connections compared to the data center network. Furthermore, ensuring security, integrity, and robustness is paramount.

Given the outlook that federated learning has drawn regarding computational scalability and privacy protection for machine learning applications, especially in the area of edge computing and the Internet of Things, it's not hard to predict an increase in the number of clients. In order to keep the pace, handling the challenges this increase would cause is mandatory.

Although the possibility of keeping data preserved at their production location by favor of FL, reduces the communication cost profoundly, still there are some overheads that can be annoying especially in the presence of a very high amount of clients. In order to efficiently model convergence by aggregator, several rounds of model update must be run. Following challenges force the aggregator to lengthen each round or increase the needed round. In each case the communication rises and the training phase would take longer.

2.4.1.3.1   Uneven Distribution of Data among Clients

In Federated Learning, there's no guarantee that data from different clients will be evenly distributed or share the same characteristics. This phenomenon, known as "non-independently and identically distributed data" or Non-IID, is common in real-world situations. It means that data from various clients (devices) might not follow the same distribution or could be interdependent due to unique behaviors and environments. This variability is a significant challenge in Federated Learning, as each client contributes data influenced by their specific context. Non-IID data contributes to communication costs in Federated Learning in several ways. The ways include increased model updates, frequent synchronization, slower convergence speed, and data skewness.

Increased model updates occur because each client, having a unique data distribution, will likely produce a distinct model update during training. The server needs to aggregate updates from all clients, leading to increased communication. To address these updates, synchronization is often needed. Frequent synchronization becomes necessary because the model parameters can diverge significantly across clients due to the non-IID nature of the data. To prevent this, more frequent communication between the server and clients is required, increasing the communication cost. It should be noted that convergence speed is also impacted. Non-IID data can slow down the convergence of the model, requiring more communication rounds to reach the desired accuracy. In addition to convergence challenges, data skewness emerges as a critical issue. Some classes of data may be over-represented in some clients and under-represented in others in non-IID settings. This imbalance can lead to poor model performance, requiring additional communication to correct.

2.4.1.3.2 Variability in Clients Connections

This issue arises in cellular networks where devices connect with varying signal strengths due to their geographical locations and environmental conditions. Devices with poor connectivity can hinder the training process by slowing it down.

2.4.2 Solutions

This section examines some solutions provided for critical challenges outlined in this section.

2.4.2.1 Solutions for Data Heterogeneity and Skewed Client Participation

As mentioned earlier, a well-designed aggregator is crucial in addressing two significant challenges in federated learning: heterogeneous data across clients and skewed client participation.

2.4.2.1.1 Strategies to Mitigate Data Heterogeneity

Data heterogeneity can be mitigated with advanced aggregation algorithms, client clustering, and robust statistical methods [14].

1. **Advanced Aggregation Algorithms**: Federated Averaging (FedAvg), which is specially designed to handle independently and identically distributed non-IID data, can provide assistance. The algorithms normalize the influence of diverse data sets by weighing the contributions of each client according to the quality or quantity of their data.
2. **Client Clustering**: Grouping clients with similar data characteristics together before aggregation can also mitigate heterogeneity. Within these clusters, models are trained locally on more homogeneous data, and the results are aggregated separately before a final global aggregation.
3. **Robust Statistical Techniques**: Applying techniques like outlier detection to discard or reweight updates that are too far from the mean or median can prevent extreme values from skewing the model.

Table 2.5 summarizes mentioned strategies to mitigate data heterogeneity.

2.4.2.1.2 Strategies to Mitigate Skewed Client Participation

In order to mitigate skewed client participation, incentive mechanisms are used as well as periodic rebalancing in order to select more fair clients [14].

1. **Fair Client Selection**: Implementing a fair client selection protocol that ensures all clients have equal chances of participation over time. This can include mechanisms to track participation history and adjust probabilities accordingly.
2. **Incentive Mechanisms**: Providing incentives for underrepresented clients to participate can balance the participation rates across the network.
3. **Periodic Rebalancing**: Periodically adjusting the model to account for underrepresented client data by either boosting their model updates or explicitly promoting their participation.

Table 2.6 summarizes mentioned strategies to mitigate skewed client participation.

2.4.2.1.3   Strategies for Mitigating Communication Problems

To tackle this challenge, two main approaches are used: reducing the size of the update model and carefully selecting which clients participate in the training process. Reducing the size of the update model in federated learning involves strategies to minimize the data transferred from individual clients to the central server during model training, and for reduction, there are three common ways which are quantization, sparsification, and gradient compression.

Quantization reduces the precision of model parameters by converting them to lower-bit representations. By using fewer bits to represent each parameter, quantization reduces the amount of data transferred without severely impacting model

Table 2.5 Strategies to mitigate data heterogeneity

Strategy	Description	Benefit
Advanced aggregation algorithms	Algorithms that weight client updates differently based on data characteristics	Ensures fair representation in the global model
Client clustering	Grouping similar clients for localized aggregation	Reduces the impact of data variability
Robust statistical techniques	Techniques to handle outliers in data updates	Prevents extreme data from skewing results

Table 2.6 Strategies to mitigate skewed client participation

Strategy	Description	Benefit
Fair client selection	A selection protocol that ensures equal participation opportunities	Reduces bias in model training
Incentive mechanisms	Incentives for increased participation from underrepresented clients	Balances the training data pool
Periodic rebalancing	Adjustments to include underrepresented data	Enhances model fairness and accuracy

performance. Developing aggregation techniques that are resilient to the impacts of quantization is an emerging area of research. Sparsification involves transmitting only a subset of the most significant parameters, specifically those with the largest changes. This strategy significantly reduces data volume by focusing on the most impactful updates. In this context, adaptive sparsification is a recognized practice, requiring an automatic trade-off between efficient communication and the model's optimality. Gradient compression, similar to sparsification, compresses the gradients (the derivative of the loss function with respect to model parameters) before sending them to the central server. This may involve thresholding (sending only gradients above a certain value) or using more efficient encoding techniques to reduce data size.

It should be noted that references [15, 16] can be a great help for deeper understanding of model reduction techniques.

In Federated Learning, clients, like smartphones, IoT devices, or computers, work together to train a shared model, but each client has varying connectivity and resources. Client selection in Federated Learning is a strategy used to manage the impact of connection variability among clients. One effective approach is importance-based selection, where clients are chosen based on their contribution to the model's learning process, prioritizing those with high-quality, diverse data. Resource-aware selection focuses on clients with sufficient bandwidth and battery life, reducing interruptions and inefficiencies caused by resource constraints. Randomized selection ensures fairness and prevents overfitting by selecting clients randomly, although it may not always optimize communication efficiency.

Cluster-based selection groups clients based on attributes such as geographic proximity or data similarity, balancing the communication load and ensuring diverse data representation. Adaptive selection dynamically adjusts the client selection strategy based on real-time network conditions and client behavior, optimizing communication efficiency and robustness. Quota-based selection assigns participation quotas to clients, distributing the communication load evenly and ensuring sustainable client engagement over time.

Performance-based selection favors clients with higher computational power and consistent performance, enhancing overall training efficiency. Proximity-based selection reduces latency by choosing clients closer in physical or network proximity, improving communication efficiency and reducing data transfer issues. By employing these client selection techniques, federated learning systems can address communication challenges, leading to more efficient and effective distributed model training. Following table summarizes these strategies (Table 2.7):

2.5   Federated Learning Threats and Solutions

This section explores the security risks associated with federated learning and strategies to mitigate them for better robustness and privacy assurance.

Table 2.7 Strategies for mitigating communication problems

Class	Strategies	Description
Reduction	Quantization	Reduces the precision of model parameters, converting them to lower-bit representations to minimize data transferred. Aggregation techniques resilient to quantization impacts are being researched.
	Sparsification	Transmits only a subset of significant parameters, reducing data volume by focusing on the most impactful updates. Adaptive sparsification establishes a trade-off between communication efficiency and model optimality.
	Gradient compression	Compresses gradients before sending to the central server, using techniques like thresholding or efficient encoding to reduce data size.
Selection	Importance-based selection	Selects clients based on their data's contribution to the model's learning process, prioritizing high-quality, diverse data.
	Resource-aware selection	Focuses on clients with sufficient bandwidth and battery life to reduce interruptions and inefficiencies.
	Randomized selection	Ensures fairness and prevents overfitting by selecting clients randomly, though it may not optimize communication efficiency.
	Cluster-based selection	Groups clients based on attributes like geographic proximity or data similarity, balancing communication load and ensuring diverse data representation.
	Adaptive selection	Dynamically adjusts client selection strategy based on real-time network conditions and client behavior, optimizing communication efficiency and robustness.
	Quota-based selection	Assigns participation quotas to clients, distributing communication load evenly and ensuring sustainable client engagement over time.
	Performance-based selection	Favors clients with higher computational power and consistent performance, enhancing overall training efficiency.
	Proximity-based selection	Reduces latency by choosing clients closer in physical or network proximity, improving communication efficiency and reducing data transfer issues.

2.5.1   Security and Privacy Threats

This subsection elaborates on security and privacy threats related to federated learning.

2.5.1.1   Data Leakage

Given that Federated Learning involves sharing model updates while keeping client data on local devices, robust protocols are needed to protect sensitive information and facilitate secure communication.

In Federated Learning, clients compute local gradients based on their data and share them with a central server to update a global model. However, even though the raw data remains on the clients, gradients can still leak information about the data's characteristics, allowing adversaries to make inferences about individual users or groups.

Attackers could analyze gradients to deduce specific data points, compromising user privacy. For example, by observing patterns in the gradients, attackers might infer personal information like location, health status, or even specific records [17].

2.5.1.2   Membership Inference Attacks

In this type of attack, adversaries determine whether specific data is part of the dataset used to train the model. This can lead to significant privacy concerns, as it may reveal sensitive information about individuals or groups [17].

2.5.1.3   Model Inversion Attacks

Attackers use gradients to reconstruct input data or infer attributes of the underlying dataset. This can be a severe privacy threat, allowing adversaries to reverse-engineer private information from the gradients [17].

2.5.1.4   Adversarial Attacks

Malicious clients can inject corrupted gradients to manipulate the learning process. This can lead to model poisoning, where the entire model is compromised, affecting its performance and accuracy [17].

2.5.2   Solution of Threats

To mitigate these risks, Federated Learning systems must incorporate robust security and privacy measures, including:

2.5.2.1   Secure Aggregation

Techniques that allow the central server to aggregate gradients without learning individual contributions help reduce the risk of data leakage. It means the data can be processed while it remains ciphered. One of the key tools for this kind of computing is homomorphic encryption. This technique enables computations on encrypted data, allowing gradients to be shared without exposing their content. That's where the terms "homomorphic" come from; the relationship between the transformed data is just exactly the same as the original one [17].

2.5.2.2   Differential Privacy

Adding controlled noise to gradients can obscure specific data points, enhancing privacy and reducing the impact of membership inference attacks. Differential privacy introduces a privacy budget, which represents the level of privacy in a system, with smaller budgets indicating higher privacy. It can be implemented through noise injection, gradient clipping, and secure aggregation, balancing privacy with model utility. However, challenges include balancing privacy with model accuracy and managing computational complexity. Despite these challenges, differential privacy is a fundamental method for ensuring privacy in Federated Learning [17].

2.5.2.3   Robustness to Adversarial Attacks

Implementing checks and validations to ensure that malicious gradients don't compromise the model. This might include outlier detection or secure protocols for model updates. Robust optimization and Byzantine-Resilient Algorithms are key techniques to secure model aggregation against malicious updates by adversaries.. Robust optimization focuses on maintaining stable and reliable model performance despite variability in data or parameters. It involves techniques like uncertainty sets, regularization, and stochastic optimization to create models that can adapt to changing conditions without degrading in performance. Byzantine-resilient algorithms, on the other hand, are designed to withstand attacks from malicious clients, known as Byzantine faults. These algorithms aim to ensure the integrity of the learning process even when some clients submit corrupted or malicious data. Byzantine-resilient algorithms typically include mechanisms for secure aggregation, anomaly detection, and robust consensus to prevent malicious inputs from compromising the model's accuracy or security [17].

2.6   Federated Learning Terminology

For clarity, precision, and standardization of concepts within the federated learning concept, the following section provides terminology of federated learning.

2.6.1   Underrepresented Clients

In the context of federated learning, "Underrepresented Clients" refers to participants in the network whose data or contributions are not as frequently included or considered in the model training process as others. This underrepresentation can occur due to various reasons, such as less frequent selection for training rounds, lower data volume, or data that is significantly different from the majority of participants. Underrepresentation can lead to biases in the model, as it may not learn well from the diverse data scenarios it will encounter in actual use. Similar phrases and terms include: minority clients, which emphasizes that these clients are in the minority in terms of data contribution or selection frequency; infrequently selected clients, explicitly referring to the selection mechanism that leads to fewer opportunities for some clients to participate; marginalized clients, often used in sociopolitical contexts, describing clients whose data contributions are given less importance in the aggregation process; less active clients, referring to clients that either opt to participate less frequently or are chosen less often due to the nature of their data or network constraints; and peripheral clients, suggesting these clients are on the periphery of the main activity in the federated learning system, not central to the model updates.

2.6.2   Non-independent and Identically Distributed

In federated learning, each client's data may have unique characteristics—for example, different underlying distributions, varying degrees of label imbalance, or domain-specific patterns—leading to what is known as Non-Independent and Identically Distributed data. Unlike a traditional, centralized training scenario where data can be shuffled or balanced to achieve a more uniform distribution, federated learning must respect each client's local data constraints. This inherent heterogeneity means that the data from one client may not only be unrepresentative of another client's data, but may also differ significantly in terms of features, data quantity, and underlying statistical properties. As a result, training a robust global model becomes more challenging, since strategies that assume homogeneous data distributions often fail to generalize well across clients with varying data characteristics. Effectively addressing these non-IID conditions often requires specialized aggregation rules, personalization techniques, and sophisticated model architectures capable of accommodating and leveraging the diversity of client data.

2.6.3   Aggregator

In federated learning, the Aggregator, often a central coordinating entity such as a server or distributed service, orchestrates the iterative process of model training. Its primary functions include collecting local updates, integrating updates, and distributing the global model.

The aggregator collects model updates, such as weight parameters, gradients, or other attributes, from participating clients after each round of local training. These updates encapsulate the learned patterns from the clients' local datasets. Next, the aggregater integrates these updates using strategies that range from simple averaging to advanced methods. These strategies might weigh updates based on factors like client reliability, data quality, or model divergence, merging the updates into a single, improved global model.

Once the new global model is created, the Aggregator distributes it back to the clients for the next round of local training, ensuring that all participants access the most up-to-date, collectively learned model parameters. By managing this flow of information and continually refining the global model, the Aggregator supports privacy-preserving federated learning by achieving a collective model without accessing any individual client's raw data.

2.7 Summary

In the chapter Core Concepts of Federated Learning, we explored the foundational elements that underpin federated learning systems. The discussion began with an examination of the Key Components of Federated Learning Systems. It highlighted essential elements such as clients, servers, local models, and the global aggregation process. These components form the backbone of any federated learning system, ensuring decentralized learning while preserving data privacy.

Next, we provided An Overview of Key Components of Federated Learning. This chapter detailed synchronization strategies and coordination mechanisms that are vital for maintaining efficiency and coherence in distributed learning environments. This section emphasized the importance of communication protocols, model update timing, and client-server collaboration in ensuring successful federated learning operations.

The chapter also addressed Federated Learning Challenges and Solutions, focusing on common issues such as data heterogeneity, communication overhead, and system scalability. Proposed solutions included adaptive learning rates, client selection techniques, and model compression methods to tackle these challenges effectively.

Finally, this chapter discussed Federated Learning Threats and Solutions, examining potential security and privacy risks, such as data leakage, model poisoning, and adversarial attacks. Countermeasures like secure multiparty computation, differential privacy, and robust aggregation techniques were presented to mitigate these threats.

Through this chapter, readers gain a comprehensive understanding of the core concepts, challenges, and solutions integral to federated learning. This lays the groundwork for its application in diverse domains.

2.8 Conclusion

This chapter encapsulates the essential aspects of federated learning by highlighting the relationship between its key components and workflow. It also illustrates the innovative approach to data collaboration. It emphasizes the pivotal role of federated algorithms in efficient and scalable training. This chapter sheds light on the critical threats to federated systems and the necessity of robust security mechanisms to ensure their integrity and privacy. As a result, these insights provide a solid foundation for advancing distributed learning research and implementation.

References

1. Beltrán, E. T. M., Pérez, M. Q., Sánchez, P. M. S., Bernal, S. L., Bovet, G., Pérez, M. G., et al. (2023). Decentralized federated learning: Fundamentals, state of the art, frameworks, trends, and challenges. *IEEE Communications Surveys & Tutorials*.
2. Banabilah, S., Aloqaily, M., Alsayed, E., Malik, N., & Jararweh, Y. (2022). Federated learning review: Fundamentals, enabling technologies, and future applications. *Information Processing & Management, 59*(6), 103061.
3. Agrawal, S., Sarkar, S., Aouedi, O., Yenduri, G., Piamrat, K., Alazab, M., et al. (2022). Federated learning for intrusion detection system: Concepts, challenges and future directions. *Computer Communications, 195*, 346–361.
4. Blanco-Justicia, A., Domingo-Ferrer, J., Martínez, S., Sánchez, D., Flanagan, A., & Tan, K. E. (2021). Achieving security and privacy in federated learning systems: Survey, research challenges and future directions. *Engineering Applications of Artificial Intelligence, 106*, 104468.
5. Mothukuri, V., Parizi, R. M., Pouriyeh, S., Huang, Y., Dehghantanha, A., & Srivastava, G. (2021). A survey on security and privacy of federated learning. *Future Generation Computer Systems, 115*, 619–640.
6. McMahan, B., Moore, E., Ramage, D., Hampson, S., & y Arcas, B. A. (2017, April). Communication-efficient learning of deep networks from decentralized data. In *Artificial intelligence and statistics* (pp. 1273–1282). PMLR.
7. Zhu, H., Xu, J., Liu, S., & Jin, Y. (2021). Federated learning on non-IID data: A survey. *Neurocomputing, 465*, 371–390.
8. Li, T., Sahu, A. K., Zaheer, M., Sanjabi, M., Talwalkar, A., & Smith, V. (2020). Federated optimization in heterogeneous networks. *Proceedings of Machine Learning and Systems, 2*, 429–450.
9. Aledhari, M., Razzak, R., Parizi, R. M., & Saeed, F. (2020). Federated learning: A survey on enabling technologies, protocols, and applications. *IEEE Access, 8*, 140699–140725.
10. Khan, A., Thij, M. T., & Wilbik, A. (2022). Vertical federated learning: A structured literature review. *arXiv preprint*, arXiv:2212.00622
11. Nguyen, D. C., Ding, M., Pathirana, P. N., Seneviratne, A., Li, J., & Poor, H. V. (2021). Federated learning for internet of things: A comprehensive survey. *IEEE Communications Surveys & Tutorials, 23*(3), 1622–1658.
12. Khan, Q. W., Khan, A. N., Rizwan, A., Ahmad, R., Khan, S., & Kim, D. H. (2023). Decentralized machine learning training: A survey on synchronization, consolidation, and topologies. *IEEE Access, 11*, 68031–68050.

13. Kairouz, P., McMahan, H. B., Avent, B., Bellet, A., Bennis, M., Bhagoji, A. N., et al. (2021). Advances and open problems in federated learning. *Foundations and Trends® in Machine Learning, 14*(1–2), 1–210.
14. Zuech, R., Khoshgoftaar, T. M., & Wald, R. (2015). Intrusion detection and big heterogeneous data: A survey. *Journal of Big Data, 2*, 1–41.
15. Yang, T. J., Xiao, Y., Motta, G., Beaufays, F., Mathews, R., & Chen, M. (2023, June). Online model compression for federated learning with large models. In *ICASSP 2023–2023 IEEE International Conference on Acoustics, Speech and Signal Processing (ICASSP)* (pp. 1–5). IEEE.
16. Choudhary, T., Mishra, V., Goswami, A., & Sarangapani, J. (2020). A comprehensive survey on model compression and acceleration. *Artificial Intelligence Review, 53*, 5113–5155.
17. Zhang, J., Zhu, H., Wang, F., Zhao, J., Xu, Q., & Li, H. (2022). Security and privacy threats to federated learning: Issues, methods, and challenges. *Security and Communication Networks, 2022*(1), 2886795.

Chapter 3
Fundamentals of Cybersecurity

3.1 Introduction

Cybersecurity is the technological processes that keep valuable data and software resources safe from unauthorized access, damage, theft, and other malicious activities. The cybersecurity landscape continues to evolve every year as cyber threats continue to evolve, from traditional methods to sophisticated attacks. This evolution is due to the increasing intersection of nation-state actors, organized cybercriminal groups, and hackers. Current cyber security trends include core components such as threat detection, ransomware promotion, and attack launch. This trend has targeted threats to the infrastructure provided in cloud services and the Internet of Things (IoT). Every year, the cyber security landscape also undergoes extensive changes and developments with the increasing development of cyber criminal tools, such as viruses, phishing, spam and insider exploits and external threats that appear over wide-area networks such as the Internet. The main goal in cyber security is to protect computers, networks, systems and data from cyber threats and unauthorized access. This includes protecting the confidentiality, integrity and availability of sensitive information and digital assets against theft, damage or misuse by malicious actors. In a computer system, failure to consider cyber security causes the security and protection of related or generated data in a system not to be maintained, the system does not maintain its continuity due to disruptions caused by cyber attacks and faces operational disruptions. Failure to consider cyber security will reduce the credibility of an organization and the loss of customer trust and indescribable financial consequences. In general, cyber security goals can be stated as the CIA triad which is confidentiality, integrity, and availability. These principles complement each other and cannot be omitted. The principles of confidentiality, integrity, and availability form the foundation of cybersecurity. They are critical to protecting sensitive information and ensuring systems and networks operate correctly [1].

H. Tabrizchi, A. Aghasi, *Federated Cyber Intelligence*, SpringerBriefs in
Computer Science, https://doi.org/10.1007/978-3-031-86592-3_3

This chapter aims to introduce the fundamentals of cybersecurity. This chapter will explain the cyber security landscape, cyber security principles, key concepts and terms, types of cyber attacks and cyber security intelligence.

3.2 The Cybersecurity Landscape

The evolution of the cyber security landscape can be seen since the birth of the Internet. In short, the important cyber events of the last few decades can be expressed like this. In the early days of computing in the 1970s and 1980s, cybersecurity was not a major concern. Computers were isolated and used mainly by government and research institutions. ARPANET, the forerunner of the Internet, saw the first documented cyber incident in 1971, when Bob Thomas created the "Creeper" program, a self-replicating piece of software that showed vulnerabilities but did no harm. On the other hand, when societies faced the massive expansion of personal computers in the 1980s, the first viruses and worms appeared, such as the Brain virus of 1986 and the Morris Worm of 1988, which caused major disruptions. These early threats were often created by hobbyists and were relatively unsophisticated. Gradually, in the 1990s, societies witnessed the commercialization of the Internet. This commercialization process itself led to an increase in cyber crimes. The advent of the World Wide Web brought more users online and with them a new generation of cyber threats. The first large-scale cyber attacks, such as the Melissa virus in 1999, demonstrated the potential for widespread damage. The 2000s marked the era of professional cybercrime. Organized crime syndicates recognized the financial potential of cyber attacks, leading to the proliferation of phishing, ransomware and identity theft schemes. Notable incidents include the 2007 cyberattacks on Estonia, which highlighted the potential for state-sponsored cyber warfare. In the 2010s, people witnessed the increase in the frequency and complexity of cyber threats. High-profile breaches, such as the 2013 Target breach and the 2017 Equifax breach, exposed the personal information of millions of people [2].

In today's world, the current cybersecurity landscape is shaped by several key trends. One of the main trends is the increasing use of artificial intelligence (AI) and machine learning in setting up or defending against cyber attacks. AI can help detect and respond to threats faster, but attackers can also use it to automate and improve their strategies. On the other hand, there is an increasing focus on trustless security models. In a zero-trust framework, organizations automatically trust no entity, whether inside or outside their network, and continuously authenticate everything that tries to connect to their systems. This approach helps reduce the risk of insider threats and lateral movement in a network. In recent years, the rise of remote work, accelerated by the Covid-19 pandemic, has also had a profound impact on cyber security. With more employees working from home, organizations must secure a wider range of devices and networks, leading to increased investment in virtual private networks (VPNs), endpoint security, and secure access service edge (SASE) solutions. Finally, the threat landscape is perceived to continue to evolve with the increasing prevalence of supply chain attacks, where adversaries target less secure elements of an organization's supply chain to gain access to their primary targets. Current cyber security trends include core components such as threat detection, ransomware promotion, and attack launch. This trend has targeted threats to the infrastructure provided in cloud services and the Internet of Things (IoT). Every year, the cyber security landscape also undergoes extensive changes and developments with the increasing development of cyber criminal tools, such as viruses, phishing, spam and insider exploits [1, 2].

3.3   Principles of Cybersecurity

A fundamental principle of cyber security is the CIA triad, which stands for confidentiality, integrity, and availability. The principles provide a framework for managing and protecting sensitive information. Each component of the triad addresses a specific aspect of security in an effort to ensure that information is secure, accurate, and is available to authorized individuals only [1]. Figure 3.1 provides an illustration of the CIA triad.

3.3.1   Confidentiality

The concept of confidentiality refers to the protection of information against unauthorized access and disclosure. This principle ensures that sensitive data can only be accessed by authorized individuals or systems. In order to maintain confidentiality,

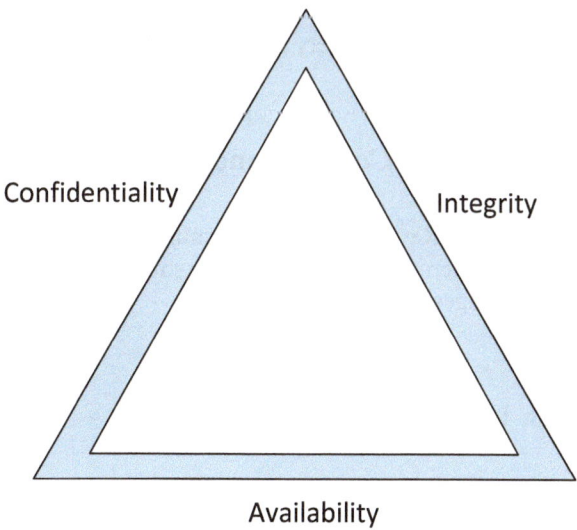

Fig. 3.1 The illustration of CIA triad

there are a number of methods that can be used. These methods include encryption, access control, and multi-factor authentication. There are a number of potential vulnerabilities that can compromise the confidentiality of a user, such as phishing attacks, weak passwords, and unpatched software.

3.3.2   Integrity

Data integrity ensures that data is accurate and complete throughout its lifecycle. It involves protecting data from alteration by unauthorized entities, ensuring its integrity and non-modification. There are several steps that can be taken to ensure the integrity of data, such as checksums, hash functions, digital signatures, and access control and auditing. The most common threats to integrity are malware, SQL injection attacks, and physical tampering. Data integrity can be maintained by implementing regular backups, data validation techniques, and monitoring of file integrity, all of which are essential practices for ensuring data integrity.

3.3.3   Availability

Availability ensures that data and systems are accessible to authorized users whenever needed. This principle is crucial for maintaining information systems' functionality, especially in critical environments such as healthcare and finance. Vulnerabilities that affect availability include distributed denial of service (DDoS) attacks, hardware failures, and ransomware. To maintain high availability, it is crucial to have effective DDoS protection tools, to maintain up-to-date hardware, as well as to have a robust disaster recovery plan in place.

3.4   Cybersecurity Key Concepts and Terminology

The section Cybersecurity Key Concepts and Terminology introduces foundational principles and essential terms in cybersecurity, laying the foundation for understanding threats, challenges, and strategies.

3.4.1   Threats, Vulnerabilities, and Risks

Cybersecurity and risk management primarily require consideration of threats, vulnerabilities, and risks. By understanding these concepts, organizations can implement effective security measures. In general, identifying vulnerabilities and

assessing the threats associated with them lead to reducing risks. Threats, vulnerabilities, and risks are explained below [1, 3].

- **Threat**: The term threat refers to any circumstance or event that can negatively affect operations, assets, individuals, or other organizations through unauthorized access, destruction, disclosure, modification, or denial of service. Threats can harm systems or organizations by causing unwanted incidents. Threats, in other words, represent the possibility of exploiting a vulnerability to compromise security and cause harm. A threat can be intentional, like hacking attempts, or unintentional, like natural disasters. Potentially harmful external or internal factors.
- **Vulnerability**: In terms of security, a vulnerability is a weakness in a system, procedure, design, implementation, or internal control that could be exploited by a threat source. According to formal definitions, it is the condition of being vulnerable to attack or harm caused by gaps or weaknesses in protective measures. Vulnerabilities, in other words, are weaknesses or gaps in security that can be exploited by threats to gain unauthorized access to an asset. Misconfigurations, lack of encryption, or even human error can cause these problems.
- **Risk**: When a threat exploits a vulnerability, an asset is potentially lost, damaged, or destroyed. Essentially, risk refers to the likelihood that a given threat source will exploit a vulnerability and its impact on an organization. When vulnerabilities are exploited, risks arise. An assessment of risk involves identifying vulnerabilities, analyzing threats, and determining their potential consequences.

Table 3.1 provides a practical context for each term and provides further details for better understanding.

In cybersecurity, the combination of Threat, Vulnerability, and Risk is often encapsulated in a concept known as the "Risk Model". In the model below, these three factors are shown in relation to how they interact to quantify and manage potential security concerns. In fact, risk is a function of threats exploiting vulnerabilities to cause potential harm or loss. Which can be mathematically expressed as:

$$Risk = Threat \times Vulnerability \times Impact$$

To mitigate risks, organizations can use this equation to assess the likelihood and impact of potential security incidents. An organization's risk can be identified and evaluated using the Risk Equation. The key to assessing security posture is to understand threats, vulnerabilities, and impacts. By assigning values to various risk components, organizations can compare risks more objectively.

Table 3.2 shows how federated learning can improve threat detection, vulnerability assessment, and risk management by enhancing cybersecurity.

Cybersecurity can be enhanced by federated learning through improved threat detection, vulnerability assessment, and risk management, if data privacy, model poisoning, and communication overhead are taken into consideration.

Table 3.1 Threats, vulnerabilities, and risks

Category	Definition	Key characteristics	Examples
Threat	Any circumstance or event that can negatively affect operations, assets, or individuals through unauthorized access, destruction, disclosure, modification, or denial of service.	– Can be intentional (e.g., hacking) or unintentional (e.g., natural disasters). – Exploits vulnerabilities.	Hacking attempts, malware, insider threats, earthquakes.
Vulnerability	A weakness in a system, procedure, design, or internal control that could be exploited by a threat source to gain unauthorized access, damage assets, or disrupt services.	– Represents gaps in security. – May result from misconfigurations, lack of encryption, or human error.	Unpatched software, weak passwords, improper access controls.
Risk	The likelihood and impact of a threat exploiting a vulnerability, potentially leading to loss, damage, or destruction of assets or systems.	– Depends on the combination of threats and vulnerabilities. – Involves assessment of likelihood and impact.	Data breaches from phishing attacks, server downtime due to DDoS attacks.

3.4.2   Cyber Attacks and Attackers

Cyber attacks are deliberate attempts to exploit computer systems, networks, and enterprises. Cybercriminals alter computer code, logic, or data using malicious code, resulting in disruptions and breaches of data. The next section describes each cyber attack mentioned below in more detail [3, 4].

1. **Malware Attack**: Involves malicious software like viruses, worms, trojans, and ransomware that damage or disable systems.
2. **The Phishing Attack:** A method of tricking individuals into providing sensitive information through deceptive communication, such as emails.
3. **Denial-of-Service (DoS) Attack**: Overloads systems, networks, or servers to prevent legitimate access.
4. **Man-in-the-Middle (MitM) Attack**: Eavesdropping attack where the attacker intercepts communication between two parties.
5. **SQL Injection Attack**: Insertion of malicious SQL code into a database query to manipulate data.
6. **Zero-Day Exploit**: Attacks that occur on the same day a weakness is discovered, before a fix is available.
7. **Password Attack**: Methods like brute-force or dictionary attacks to gain unauthorized access by cracking passwords.
8. **Cross-Site Scripting (XSS)**: Injection of malicious scripts into trusted websites' content.

Table 3.2 Threat detection, vulnerability assessment, and risk management

Category	Role of federated learning	Key benefits	Challenges and considerations
Threat detection	• Federated learning enables collaborative training on diverse datasets without sharing sensitive data. • Develops robust models for identifying emerging threats effectively. • Facilitates rapid sharing of threat intelligence across organizations.	• Enhanced detection capabilities. • Real-time threat intelligence sharing. • Reduced false positives/negatives.	• Data quality and privacy must be ensured. • FL models can be vulnerable to poisoning attacks.
Vulnerability assessment	• Federated learning analyzes data from various sources to identify unknown vulnerabilities and monitor systems continuously. • Aggregates data to prioritize critical vulnerabilities and allocate resources effectively. • Provides timely insights for patching and mitigating new vulnerabilities.	• Identifies previously unknown vulnerabilities. • Prioritizes critical vulnerabilities. • Enables continuous vulnerability monitoring.	• Communication overhead due to frequent interactions between devices.
Risk management	• Federated learning assesses risk exposure by analyzing data from multiple sources and identifying potential threats. • Provides insights for informed decision-making and resource prioritization. • Enhances incident response by enabling faster identification and analysis of security incidents.	• Improves risk assessment through broader data analysis. • Enables data-driven decision-making. • Enhances incident response.	• Effective resource allocation is necessary to mitigate potential communication delays.

Understanding attack types and attackers is equivalent to knowing our enemy. In this way, a cyberattack can be expected, effectively defended against, and its damage minimized. There are various types of attackers, each with distinct motivations. Cybercriminals typically act for financial gain, while hacktivists focus on advancing political or social causes. State-sponsored hackers, often backed by governments, engage in espionage or sabotage. Insider threats arise when employees or associates misuse their access privileges. Script kiddies, though inexperienced, use existing tools to seek thrills or gain recognition. Finally, cyber terrorists aim to instill fear or disrupt systems on a large scale. The following table illustrates types of attackers, their motivation, and common attack methods, and descriptions of their work processes (Table 3.3).

Table 3.3 Types of attackers, their motivation, and common attack methods

Type of attacker	Motivation	Common attacks	Description
Cybercriminals	Financial gain	Malware, phishing, ransomware	Seek monetary benefits by stealing data, extorting money, or fraud. Operate individually or as part of organized crime groups.
Hacktivists	Ideological	DDoS, website defacement	Promote political or social causes. Attack targets that oppose their beliefs to bring attention to their agenda.
State-sponsored hackers	Espionage/ sabotage	Advanced persistent threats	Backed by governments to steal sensitive information, disrupt services, or damage infrastructure of other nations or organizations.
Insider threats	Personal motives	Data theft, sabotage	Authorized individuals misuse access. Motivated by revenge, greed, or negligence. Can be employees, contractors, or business partners.
Script kiddies	Curiosity/ recognition	Website defacement, DoS	Novices using existing tools or scripts without deep understanding. Seek thrill or notoriety rather than significant harm.
Cyber terrorists	Fear/ disruption	Infrastructure attacks	Use cyber means to cause panic, fear, or disrupt critical services. Target national security, economy, or public safety.

3.4.3 Assets, Controls, and Countermeasures

The three components of cybersecurity and risk management are assets, controls, and countermeasures. In a nutshell, assets are what organizations want to protect, controls represent how they protect them, and countermeasures represent the ways in which those controls are implemented in order to defend against identified threats [5]. Creating a robust cyber defense requires a comprehensive understanding of all three, as shown in Fig. 3.2.

3.4.3.1 Assets

Assets are anything that is valuable to an organization and needs to be protected. This includes physical items such as hardware and facilities, as well as non-physical items like data and intellectual property. An asset is a valuable resource that needs to be safeguarded from threats [5]. In terms of security, assets are the primary focus. In general, they can be categorized as shown in Table 3.4:

It should be noted that asset protection involves understanding their value and the impact of their loss.

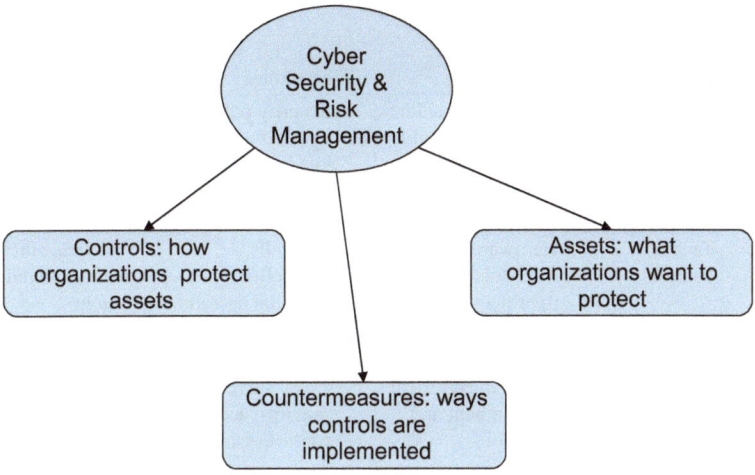

Fig. 3.2 Assets, controls, and countermeasures

Table 3.4 Assets

Asset category	Description	Examples	Significance
Physical assets	Tangible resources such as hardware and facilities essential for operations.	Computers, servers, network devices, office buildings.	Must be protected to ensure operational continuity and prevent physical loss or damage.
Information assets	Data and documentation that are critical for decision-making, operations, and compliance.	Customer data, databases, software documentation, trade secrets.	Vital for maintaining business operations and compliance with data protection laws.
Human assets	Personnel whose skills and knowledge are key to organizational success.	Employees, contractors, management teams.	Their expertise and integrity directly influence productivity and security.
Intangible assets	Non-physical resources that represent the organization's reputation and intellectual property.	Brand reputation, intellectual property (patents, copyrights), customer trust.	Crucial for maintaining competitive advantage and stakeholder confidence.

3.4.3.2 Controls

There are many types of controls that are designed to provide reasonable assurance that business objectives will be achieved as well as undesired events will be prevented or detected and corrected. The purpose of these mechanisms is to reduce the risk associated with the project. Assets are protected through controls that reduce vulnerabilities and mitigate risks [5]. The Table 3.5 categorizes controls based on their type and purpose.

Table 3.5 Controls

In terms of	Control type or purpose	Description	Examples	Purpose
Type	Administrative controls	Policies, procedures, training, and guidelines that govern organizational behavior and processes.	Security policies, employee training, incident response plans.	Establish a framework for secure operations and reduce human errors.
	Technical controls	Hardware and software mechanisms designed to protect systems and data.	Firewalls, encryption, intrusion detection systems (IDS).	Protect against cyber threats and reduce system vulnerabilities.
	Physical controls	Measures designed to secure the physical environment and resources.	Security guards, locks, surveillance cameras, access control systems.	Prevent unauthorized physical access to facilities and assets.
Purpose	Preventive controls	Aim to stop security incidents from occurring.	Access controls, authentication mechanisms, firewalls.	Proactively reduce the likelihood of security incidents.
	Detective controls	Identify and alert to security incidents when they occur.	Audit logs, IDS, monitoring systems.	Provide early detection of security breaches or anomalies.
	Corrective controls	Address and fix security incidents after they have occurred.	Patch management, incident response plans.	Minimize damage and restore systems to a secure state.

3.4.3.3   Countermeasures

A countermeasure is an action, device, procedure, or technique that reduces a threat, vulnerability, or attack by eliminating or preventing it, minimizing harm, or discovering and reporting it. These controls are specific implementations of controls that are designed to mitigate a specific risk in a specific way [4, 5]. There are specific actions and tools that can be used to counter threats and vulnerabilities. There are a number of examples that include the following (Table 3.6):

To ensure the integrity, confidentiality, and availability of data and models in federated learning, understanding Assets, Controls, and Countermeasures is essential. Developing effective Controls like secure aggregation and differential privacy, deploying targeted Countermeasures against specific threats, and identifying and protecting assets such as local data, models, and communication channels can enhance federated learning system security. As a result of understanding these concepts, federated learning not only achieves its goal of collaborative model training, but also maintains the trust and confidence of users by protecting their data and ensuring learning integrity. Table 3.7 summarize the description of Assets, Controls, and Countermeasures in federated learning, along with examples for each.

Table 3.6   Countermeasures

Countermeasure	Description	Purpose	Examples of mitigated risks
Installing antivirus software	A software solution that detects, prevents, and removes malware from devices and systems.	Protects systems from malware infections.	Viruses, ransomware, spyware.
Implementing Multi-Factor Authentication (MFA)	Requires multiple forms of verification before granting access to systems or data.	Reduces the risk of unauthorized access.	Compromised passwords, phishing attacks.
Regular security training	Educates employees on recognizing and responding to security threats and best practices.	Mitigates risks associated with human error.	Social engineering, phishing, accidental data leaks.

Table 3.7   Assets, controls, and countermeasures in federated learning

Component	Description	Examples in federated learning
Assets	Valuable elements that need protection within the system.	– Local data on clients – Local models and updates – Global model – Communication channels – Client devices – Privacy
Controls	Measures implemented to protect assets by reducing vulnerabilities and mitigating risks.	– Secure aggregation protocols – Differential privacy – Encryption – Authentication – Anomaly detection systems
Countermeasures	Specific actions or implementations designed to neutralize or mitigate identified threats by addressing vulnerabilities.	– Client selection strategies – Update clipping – Secure multi-party computation – Homomorphic encryption

3.5   Cyber Attacks

Individuals, businesses, and even government agencies are targets of cyber attacks in today's digital world. Typically, these attacks involve unauthorized access, manipulation, or damage to computer systems and networks. Malware, phishing, ransomware, and denial-of-service (DoS) attacks are just some of the ways cyber criminals exploit vulnerabilities. In many cases, the motives behind these attacks are varied, ranging from financial gain and personal vendettas to political influence and activism. Data breaches, financial losses, compromised privacy, and disruptions to core services can be devastating consequences of cyber attacks. Increasing digital dependency makes understanding cyberattacks and defending against them essential in today's online world [6].

3.5.1   The Motivations Behind Cyber Attacks

There are many motivations behind cyber attacks, which often reflect the diverse objectives of the attackers. Financial gain is one of the most common motives, with attackers targeting individuals, businesses, and financial institutions. This is most often done to steal funds or sensitive information that can be sold or exploited. For instance, ransomware holds critical data hostage, forcing victims to pay for its release. Identities may also be stolen and used for fraud or resale. Cryptocurrencies, which enable criminals to receive payments anonymously, have increased the profitability of these attacks. Attackers are sometimes motivated by vendettas and financial rewards. In the pursuit of revenge, disgruntled employees and former partners may target a certain person or organization to destroy their reputation.

Cyber attacks are often motivated by political influence or activism, also referred to as hacktivism. Hacktivists employ cyber tactics to raise awareness of social or political issues, challenge governments, or undermine institutions they perceive to be unethical or oppressive. As an example, they may deface websites, leak sensitive information, or launch distributed denial-of-service attacks in order to temporarily disrupt the operations of a target. Cyberattacks can sometimes be used by state-sponsored attackers as a form of espionage, aiming to gather intelligence, or applying pressure without direct conflict. This type of attack often involves stealing trade secrets, customer data, or intellectual property, allowing the attackers to improve their market position. The motives behind cyber attacks continue to diversify as technology becomes more integral to all sectors, requiring resilient and adaptive defenses.

The motives for cyber attacks can vary widely. Financial gain involves attacks aimed at stealing money, sensitive information, or using ransomware to extort payments. Personal vendetta refers to revenge-based attacks, often carried out by disgruntled employees or associates seeking to harm an individual or organization. Political influence or activism, also known as "hacktivism," includes activities aimed at promoting social or political causes, often targeting governments or organizations viewed as unethical. State-sponsored espionage involves cyber attacks funded or conducted by governments to gather intelligence or destabilize other countries. Corporate espionage refers to competitive attacks designed to steal trade secrets, customer data, or intellectual property from rival companies. Lastly, intellectual challenge describes attacks conducted for personal satisfaction, testing skills, or gaining recognition within hacker communities [6, 7].

3.5.2   Types of Cyber Attacks

A cyber attack is a set of malicious activities designed to compromise the security, integrity, and availability of a particular information system in a variety of ways. Key types of cyberattacks include malware (such as viruses, worms, trojans, and ransomware) that can corrupt or steal data, disrupt systems, and extort money from victims. Phishing and social engineering attacks exploit human psychology to trick individuals into revealing sensitive information or performing actions that compromise security. Denial of Service (DoS) and Distributed Denial of Service (DDoS) attacks aim to render systems unavailable by overwhelming them with traffic, while Man-in-the-Middle attacks intercept and alter communication between parties. Advanced Persistent Threats involve long-term, targeted attacks typically by well-resourced adversaries seeking to steal data or monitor activities over time. Lastly, zero-day exploits take advantage of undisclosed vulnerabilities, causing significant threats until patches are developed. Understanding these attack vectors is crucial for developing effective cybersecurity strategies and protecting against potential attacks [6, 7].

3.5.2.1   Malware

Malware, or malicious software as it is commonly known, is a collection of potentially harmful programs like viruses, worms, trojan horses, and ransomware. The characteristics and modes of operation of each type are unique. When legitimate files and programs are shared, viruses attach themselves to these files and spread. It is possible for them to corrupt or delete data, disrupt systems, and steal information. As worms replicate themselves, they can spread across networks without the need for user interaction, causing extensive damage and disrupting networks. After a Trojan has been activated, it reveals itself as benign software, allowing unauthorized access to or control over infected computers. A ransomware attack encrypts user data and demands payment for its decryption, with high-profile attacks targeting hospitals, corporations, and governmental organizations. Examples of notable ransomware outbreaks include WannaCry and Petya.

3.5.2.2   Phishing and Social Engineering

Human psychology is exploited rather than technical vulnerabilities in phishing and social engineering attacks. The act of phishing involves sending fraudulent communications, usually emails, that appear to come from reputable sources. These emails often contain malicious links or attachments, aiming to steal sensitive information such as login credentials, financial information, or personal data. Social engineering is a broad tactic that manipulates individuals into providing confidential information or performing actions that compromise security. Techniques include pretexting, baiting, and spear-phishing, where attackers customize their approach to specific individuals or organizations. For instance, an attacker might act as an IT support person to trick employees into revealing their passwords. Preventing these attacks requires a combination of technical defenses, such as email filtering and multi-factor authentication, and strong user education programs that teach employees to recognize and report suspicious activities.

3.5.2.3   Denial of Service (DoS) and Distributed Denial of Service (DDoS)

The purpose of a Denial of Service (DoS) attack is to make a system or network resource unavailable to users who are intended to use it by overloading it with a flood of illegitimate requests. As a result, legitimate requests cannot be processed, causing significant disruption to online services. The effect of a distributed denial of service (DDoS) attack is exacerbated by the use of multiple compromised devices, often as part of a botnet, to launch a coordinated attack. These attacks can target various layers of the network stack, with application-layer DDoS attacks being particularly challenging to mitigate. They can affect websites, email services, and even financial transactions, with attackers sometimes asking for a ransom to terminate the attack. DDoS mitigation strategies include network traffic analysis, rate limiting, and DDoS protection services.

3.5.2.4   Man-in-the-Middle Attacks

As a result of Man-in-the-Middle attacks, an attacker intercepts and potentially alters communication between two parties without their knowledge or consent. This can take various forms, including intercepting unsecured Wi-Fi communications, exploiting vulnerabilities in network protocols, or utilizing malware. An attacker may be able to monitor conversations, steal sensitive information, and inject malicious content into the communication stream. Man-in-the-Middle attacks can compromise the confidentiality and integrity of the data being exchanged. This poses significant risks to online banking, email communication, and other sensitive transactions. Defending against this type of attack involves using encryption protocols like HTTPS for secure communications, employing virtual private networks (VPNs), and ensuring that security certificates are correctly validated to prevent interception.

3.5.2.5   Advanced Persistent Threats

Cyberattacks involving advanced persistent threats are typically conducted by well-resourced, skilled attackers, which are often linked to nation states or organized crime groups. These attacks aim to gain access to and remain undetected within a target's network for extended periods, gathering intelligence or exfiltrating data. Advanced persistent threats use various techniques, including spear-phishing, zero-day exploits, and custom malware, to obtain and maintain access. When an attacker has gained access to a network, they will move laterally within the network, escalate privileges, and establish multiple points of persistence in order to make sure that they can continue to gain access even if some entry points are discovered and closed. Advanced persistent threats target high-value entities like government agencies, defense contractors, and large enterprises. Mitigating advanced persistent threats requires a multi-layered security approach, including advanced threat detection systems, regular security assessments, incident response planning, and continuous monitoring for unusual activities.

3.5.2.6   Zero-Day Exploits

The goal of zero-day exploits is to take advantage of previously unknown vulnerabilities in software, hardware, or firmware that have not yet been patched by developers. Due to the fact that these exploits are effective until the vulnerability is discovered and fixed by the vendor, they are very valuable to attackers. Often, zero-day attacks target critical infrastructure, government systems, and major corporations, causing significant damage. Zero-day exploits are used by attackers to gain unauthorized access to systems, exfiltrate data, or disrupt operations. The defense against zero-day exploits is challenging due to their unknown nature, but proactive security measures can minimize risks. This includes implementing intrusion detection and prevention systems, applying the principle of least privilege, keeping software and systems updated, and participating in threat intelligence sharing. This will enable us to stay informed about emerging threats.

3.5.3   Impact of Cyber Attacks

Cyberattacks have widespread impact on businesses, individuals, and governments, resulting in both immediate and long-term consequences. Financial losses are among the most noticeable effects, particularly for businesses and financial institutions that handle large volumes of transactions and sensitive data. Attackers can steal funds directly through fraudulent transactions, manipulate stock values, or use ransomware to demand payments in exchange for releasing critical data. This financial impact is not only immediate but can also lead to long-term losses, as affected organizations may face increased security costs and legal responsibilities. For individuals, identity theft and fraud can disrupt personal finances, leaving victims with damaged credit and long-term recovery challenges. The costs associated with such attacks are considerable, often requiring extensive time and money to resolve. In many cases, these attacks occur through phishing scams, social engineering, or other forms of deception. These attacks can happen anytime someone unknowingly reveals sensitive information or clicks on a malicious link [6, 7].

Cyber attacks also cause reputational damage, especially for businesses and governments that rely on public trust. When an organization suffers a data breach, customers may lose confidence in its ability to protect their personal information. This may result in lost clients and a tarnished brand image. For governments, the exposure of classified or sensitive information can shake public confidence, eroding trust in institutions supposed to safeguard national interests. Such breaches often come to light when attackers publicly leak sensitive data or when the organization is forced to disclose the breach due to legal obligations. Once reputation is damaged, the affected entities may struggle to regain stakeholders' trust, often requiring significant efforts in transparency, public relations, and additional security measures.

Cyberattacks also result in data breaches that compromise personal, financial, and proprietary information. The dark web is a popular place for attackers to sell customer data, from payment information to personal identification. In many cases, these breaches go undetected for months or years because attackers bypass security measures or exploit system vulnerabilities. These breaches expose companies' trade secrets and intellectual property, exposing individuals to identity theft and fraud. National security and intelligence information can also be compromised by governments, leading to diplomatic tensions and possibly threatening citizens. Often, cyber attacks occur when organizations are least prepared, making proactive cybersecurity measures essential. Due to the increasing reliance on digital technology, cyber attacks continue to evolve, making cyber security practices increasingly critical [7].

3.5.4 Stages of a Cyber Attack

A cyber attack generally follows a structured process known as the "cyber kill chain," where attackers execute their plan in a systematic sequence. By understanding each stage, organizations can spot and disrupt attacks before they cause serious damage [6, 7]. The main stages include:

- **First Stage: Reconnaissance:** In this initial phase, attackers gather information about their target, often conducting extensive research to find vulnerabilities. They might analyze employee profiles on social media or map out the target's network infrastructure. This phase is usually passive and goes undetected, helping attackers identify potential entry points and weak areas to exploit.
- **Second Stage: Weaponization:** After pinpointing vulnerabilities, attackers create or select tools designed to exploit these weaknesses. This might include malware, phishing schemes, or trojans specifically crafted for the target's environment. Weaponization often involves creating a backdoor or exploit that will later grant access to the target's systems.
- **Third Stage: Delivery:** Next, attackers deliver their weapon to the target, commonly through phishing emails, malicious attachments, or compromised websites. The delivery method can vary, but the aim is to trick the victim into unknowingly introducing malware into their network or device.
- **Fourth Stage: Exploitation:** Once delivered, the malware activates to exploit the target's vulnerabilities. This could involve executing malicious code, installing ransomware, or seizing system control. Exploitation is often automated, making it a swift and efficient process.
- **Fifth Stage: Installation:** Upon successful exploitation, attackers install malware, spyware, or other malicious software to establish a lasting presence in the

network. This step allows them to access and control systems even if the target detects an intrusion and attempts basic defenses.

- **Sixth Stage: Command and Control (C2):** Attackers then set up a command-and-control channel to monitor the compromised system. This channel enables them to issue commands, collect data, and manage malware. C2 keeps attackers connected and lets them adjust their approach as needed.
- **Seventh Stage: Actions on Objective:** In the final stage, attackers pursue their goals, such as data exfiltration, network disruption, or system sabotage. Here, they might collect sensitive data, alter system functions, or deploy ransomware. Once they achieve their objectives, attackers may cover their tracks to evade detection and prepare for future attacks.

3.5.5 Preventative Measures

Preventative measures in cybersecurity are crucial for defending against the increasingly complex landscape of cyberattacks. These measures focus on proactive strategies to protect data, systems, and networks from various threats, including malware, phishing, and other advanced persistent threats. In order to ensure a strong cybersecurity stance, an organization must assess its risks and manage vulnerabilities. Regular vulnerability assessments and penetration testing allow organizations to detect and address system flaws before attackers exploit them. Additionally, secure coding practices and thorough code reviews help prevent common software vulnerabilities attackers use. Network security measures are also key to preventing attacks. Firewalls, intrusion detection systems (IDS), and intrusion prevention systems (IPS) serve as the first line of defense, blocking unauthorized access attempts and flagging suspicious activities. Network segmentation, which divides a network into smaller, isolated sections, helps contain breaches and limit attack impact. For example, isolating critical systems or sensitive data within specific network segments reduces the risk of widespread compromise if a breach occurs. Similarly, robust authentication and access controls, such as multi-factor authentication and the principle of least privilege, restrict access to sensitive systems and information, lowering the risk of insider threats and unauthorized access. Employee training and awareness are also vital to cybersecurity strategies. Social engineering and phishing are among the most common attack methods, often exploiting human error instead of technical vulnerabilities. Regular training on recognizing phishing attempts, maintaining secure passwords, and safeguarding confidential information can significantly reduce these risks. Additionally, data encryption and regular backups ensure sensitive information remains secure in transit and at rest. This is so that even if an attacker intercepts data, they cannot easily read or misuse it. Regularly stored backups also allow quick recovery in case of ransomware attacks or data corruption. Finally, monitoring and incident response planning prepare organizations to detect suspicious activity quickly and respond accordingly. Security information and event

Table 3.8 Key preventative measures in cybersecurity

Preventative measure	Description
Risk assessment & vulnerability management	Identify and address system weaknesses through regular assessments, penetration testing, and secure coding practices.
Network security	Implement firewalls, IDS/IPS systems, and network segmentation to control and monitor access to the network.
Authentication & access control	Use multi-factor authentication and enforce the principle of least privilege to limit access to sensitive data and systems.
Employee training & awareness	Educate employees on recognizing phishing, secure password practices, and the importance of data protection.
Data encryption & regular backups	Encrypt data in transit and at rest, and perform regular backups to secure data and enable recovery after an incident.
Monitoring & incident response planning	Use tools for real-time monitoring and maintain an incident response plan for efficient breach response.

management (SIEM) tools provide real-time monitoring by correlating events across networks to identify anomalies or threats. A well-defined incident response plan, along with a trained response team, enables efficient handling of breaches, minimizing damage and ensuring quick recovery. By combining these preventative measures, organizations can establish a resilient cybersecurity defense that guards against attacks but also enables a rapid response to minimize impact if an attack occurs [8]. Table 3.8 summarize the key preventative measures in cybersecurity.

3.6 Cyber Security Intelligence

Cybersecurity Intelligence is the process of gathering, analyzing, and sharing information about potential and active cyber threats. This intelligence helps organizations understand the threat landscape, identify vulnerabilities, and develop strategies to protect against cyber attacks. Cybersecurity intelligence uses various tools and techniques to collect data from multiple sources, analyze it for patterns and trends, and transform it into actionable insights that guide security measures [9, 10].

3.6.1 Definition and Scope of Cyber Security Intelligence

The process of cybersecurity intelligence involves gathering, analyzing, and assessing information on cyber threats, vulnerabilities, and security risks. To effectively mitigate cyber threats, organizations must continuously monitor data to anticipate and respond to potential attacks. By identifying and addressing cyber risks proactively, cybersecurity intelligence helps prevent security incidents, data breaches, and damage to infrastructure.

The primary goal of cybersecurity intelligence is to detect and eliminate threats before they harm an organization, using both technological tools and human expertise. Key components of cybersecurity intelligence include:

- **Data Collection**: Gathering information from internal and external sources like security logs, public forums, and dark web marketplaces.
- **Analysis and Correlation**: Examining collected data to identify patterns, trends, and connections between threat indicators.
- **Dissemination**: Sharing relevant intelligence with stakeholders promptly to enable effective responses.
- **Actionable Intelligence**: Converting raw data into insights that guide security decisions and strengthen defenses.

The scope of Cybersecurity Intelligence includes essential functions such as data collection, analysis, correlation, and dissemination. Data collection involves gathering information from both internal systems and external sources, providing a comprehensive view of an organization's security posture. Analysis and correlation enable experts to identify relationships, trends, and behavior patterns, helping predict potential attack vectors. Dissemination ensures that relevant intelligence reaches key stakeholders in real-time, supporting prompt and informed decision-making. Cybersecurity Intelligence extends beyond simple threat detection, offering actionable insights that shape a resilient cybersecurity strategy. It not only identifies vulnerabilities but also guides incident response, compliance efforts, and strategic defense planning. Combining advanced technology with human expertise, cybersecurity intelligence is essential for strengthening defenses, anticipating threats, and fostering a proactive security approach within organizations [9, 10].

3.6.2   The Importance of Threat Data in Cyber Security Intelligence

Cybersecurity intelligence leverages threat data to identify, analyze, and mitigate cyber threats, offering actionable insights that help security teams anticipate and respond to risks. The use of high-quality threat data can help enterprises understand the evolving threat landscape, including new vulnerabilities, attack vectors, and tactics, techniques, and procedures—known as TTPs. Recognizing potential risks early allows for proactive defense strategies, enabling detection of issues before they escalate.

Security professionals can continuously collect and analyze data from diverse sources—network logs, security alerts, malware samples, and dark web activities—to identify patterns, correlate indicators of compromise, and detect malicious activity early in the attack lifecycle. This early warning capability not only prevents breaches but also enhances incident response by adding context to detected threats. As a result, organizations can prioritize resources toward the most critical threats, a crucial benefit for those with limited security resources.

Furthermore, threat data shapes long-term security policies, aiding organizations in adapting to a rapidly evolving cyber environment while supporting compliance and regulatory requirements. It also promotes collaboration within internal teams and with external partners, strengthening overall security postures and situational awareness. Ultimately, threat data in cybersecurity intelligence goes beyond threat identification; it transforms raw data into actionable intelligence that drives informed decisions, fortifies defenses, and protects organizations from both known and emerging cyber threats [9, 10].

3.6.3   Types of Cyber Threat Intelligence

In recent years, cyber threat intelligence has become one of the most important components of cybersecurity methods. It entails the collection, analysis, and dissemination of information on cyber risks. Cyber Threat Intelligence is classified into four primary forms, each serving distinct requirements.

Strategic intelligence offers a comprehensive view of the threat environment, emphasizing long-term planning and decision-making. It evaluates current trends, geopolitical influences, and threat actors' intentions. This kind of intelligence assists firms in resource allocation, long-term risk planning, and facilitates processes like budgeting and executive decision-making. Tactical intelligence emphasizes actionable knowledge about particular threats, such as malware campaigns, phishing efforts, or targeted assaults. It offers comprehensive information on attackers' methods, techniques, and processes, along with signs of compromise that indicate their existence. This kind of information facilitates threat hunting, incident response, and security operations. Operational intelligence provides immediate data on current attacks and occurrences. The emphasis is on prompt reaction and containment by addressing inquiries about the current state of the network. This includes the presence of an ongoing attack, and the measures required to mitigate its effect. This kind of intelligence is used in tools such as systems for monitoring security events, detecting intrusions, and reacting to occurrences on endpoints. Technical intelligence analyzes the exact aspects of threats, including malware, vulnerabilities, and the tools used to launch attacks. It helps companies understand the operation of these threats and identify exploitable vulnerabilities. Technical intelligence facilitates tasks like vulnerability analysis, malware reverse engineering, and research to mitigate risks [9, 10] (Table 3.9).

Organizations may improve their security by using Strategic, Tactical, Operational, and Technical Intelligence. This is for preventive detection, informed planning, and intelligent reaction to attacks.

Table 3.9 Type of cyber threat intelligence

Type of cyber threat intelligence	Purpose	Focus	Key questions
Strategic intelligence	Provides a high-level overview of the threat landscape, including emerging trends and motivations of threat actors.	Long-term planning and decision-making.	– What are the overarching trends in the threat landscape? – What are the motivations of major threat actors? – How can resources be allocated to mitigate long-term risks?
Tactical intelligence	Delivers actionable insights into specific threats, such as malware campaigns or targeted attacks.	Short-term threat response and mitigation.	– What are the TTPs used by threat actors? – What are the IOCs associated with these threats? – How can threats be detected and responded to in real-time?
Operational intelligence	Provides real-time information about ongoing attacks and incidents.	Immediate threat response and containment.	– What is happening right now in our network? – Is there an active attack underway? – What steps should we take to mitigate the attack?
Technical intelligence	Analyzes technical details of malware, vulnerabilities, and attack tools.	Understanding technical aspects of threats.	– How does this malware work? – What vulnerabilities in our systems could be exploited? – How can effective countermeasures be developed?

3.6.4 Sources of Cyber Security Intelligence

Cybersecurity intelligence is essential for protecting digital assets, and professionals rely on several key sources to gather this intelligence effectively. A key source is open-source intelligence, which involves collecting information from publicly available resources. News articles and blogs highlight emerging threats, vulnerabilities, and attack trends. Social media platforms often reveal details about threat actors, leaks, or potential vulnerabilities. Public forums and discussion boards are valuable for understanding hacking techniques, malware, and exploit kits. Code repositories can be analyzed to identify exploitable vulnerabilities in open-source software. Another significant source is the dark web and underground forums. These are hidden parts of the internet where cybercriminals communicate and trade illegal goods and services. Monitoring these forums can reveal emerging threats, attack techniques, and black market activities, such as the sale of stolen data, malware, or hacking services. Insights into cybercriminals' motivations and capabilities also help organizations prioritize security measures. Threat feeds and data-sharing platforms provide real-time updates on threats, vulnerabilities, and indicators of compromise. These include commercial feeds that aggregate data from sources such as

Table 3.10 Source of cyber security intelligence

Source of cybersecurity intelligence	Description	Key insights provided	Examples
Open Source Intelligence (OSINT)	Information gathered from publicly available sources.	– Emerging threats and vulnerabilities. – Attack trends and hacking techniques.	– News articles, blogs. – Social media. – Public forums. – Code repositories.
Dark Web and underground forums	Hidden parts of the internet where cybercriminals communicate and trade goods.	– Emerging threats and attack techniques. – Black market activities. – Threat actor motivations.	– Sale of stolen data. – Malware development. – Hacking tools and services.
Threat feeds and data sharing platforms	Real-time information from curated or shared sources about threats and vulnerabilities.	– Indicators of compromise (IOCs). – Threat trends and nation-state threats.	– Commercial threat feeds. – Government-sponsored feeds. – ISACs.
Human Intelligence (HUMINT)	Intelligence collected through human sources, expertise, and analysis.	– Insights into TTPs of attackers. – Information on vulnerabilities and zero-days.	– Security analysts. – Incident response teams. – External researchers.

malware analysis and dark web monitoring. Government-sponsored feeds provide intelligence on nation-state threats, while industry-specific information sharing and analysis centers enable collaboration among organizations in the same sector. Human intelligence also plays a crucial role. Cybersecurity analysts offer expert insights into emerging threats and vulnerabilities based on their experience. Incident response teams share information about specific attacks, including attacker tactics and techniques. External security researchers contribute valuable knowledge about emerging vulnerabilities, zero-day exploits, and advanced persistent threats [9, 10].

By combining information from these diverse sources, organizations can strengthen their ability to detect, prevent, and respond to cyber threats effectively (Table 3.10).

The combination of OSINT, Dark Web Intelligence, Threat Feeds, and HUMINT enables organizations to gain comprehensive visibility into the threat landscape, enabling proactive detection and response to cyber threats.

3.6.5 Cyber Security Intelligence Techniques

Modern security strategies include cybersecurity intelligence, which collects, analyzes, and interprets information about potential threats. To gather and analyze this intelligence, a number of key techniques are employed. One effective method is network traffic analysis, which involves monitoring and examining network communications to detect threats. This technique helps organizations identify unusual activities that may signal security breaches. It also uncovers vulnerabilities in network configurations or applications, and tracks known threat actors. Social engineering and phishing campaign analysis is another critical approach. These attacks exploit human behavior to gain unauthorized access to data or systems. By analyzing them, organizations can better understand attacker tactics, improve employee awareness, and develop targeted security training to prevent such incidents. Honeypots and deception techniques attract and distract attackers, allowing security teams to study their behavior. This method provides insights into how attackers exploit vulnerabilities. It gathers intelligence on the tools and techniques they use, and reduces the impact of attacks by diverting them from critical systems. Machine learning and artificial intelligence have revolutionized cybersecurity intelligence. These technologies automate threat detection by analyzing large data volumes. They predict future attacks using historical data, and enhance threat hunting by uncovering hidden risks. They also streamline incident response by automating processes and enabling faster threats reactions [9, 10] (Table 3.11).

Table 3.11 Cyber security intelligence techniques

Technique	Description	Key benefits	Examples
Network traffic analysis	Monitors and analyzes network communications to detect potential threats and vulnerabilities.	– Detects unusual network activity. – Identifies weaknesses in configurations. – Tracks malicious behavior.	Intrusion detection systems (IDS), anomaly detection tools.
Social engineering and phishing campaign analysis	Analyzes social engineering and phishing attacks to prevent unauthorized access.	– Identifies common attack tactics. – Improves employee awareness – Enhances security training.	Analyzing phishing emails, educating employees through simulated phishing campaigns.
Honeypots and deception techniques	Uses decoy systems and environments to lure attackers, collect intelligence, and reduce risks.	– Learns attacker methods. – Collects threat intelligence on tools and TTPs. – Diverts attackers from critical assets.	Deploying honeypots to monitor attacker behavior, setting up fake systems to detect exploits.
Machine learning and AI	Leverages advanced algorithms to enhance threat detection and response.	– Automates detection of anomalies. – Predicts future threats. – Improves incident response efficiency.	AI-driven threat hunting tools, predictive analytics systems for cybersecurity.

3.6.6 Threat Intelligence Lifecycle

The Threat Intelligence Lifecycle is a structured methodology for creating, deploying, and sustaining effective threat intelligence. It consists of six key stages. The first stage involves defining the goals and requirements of the program. This includes specifying the threats to monitor, setting intelligence priorities, and understanding the needs of stakeholders. Establishing clear objectives ensures that the program aligns with organizational goals. The second stage focuses on collecting raw data from various sources, both internal and external, as per the defined requirements. This process may include the use of automated tools, manual research, and intelligence gathered from human sources. After collection, the data enters the processing stage. This step involves cleaning, organizing, and formatting the raw data to prepare it for analysis. Irrelevant information is removed, and data from multiple sources is combined to create a unified perspective. Next, the processed data is analyzed to derive valuable insights. This phase, the most critical of all, aims to identify potential threat actors, attack methods, and vulnerabilities, turning raw data into actionable intelligence to guide decision-making. Following the analysis, the intelligence is shared with the relevant stakeholders in a timely and appropriate format. Depending on the audience, this could range from detailed technical reports for security professionals to high-level summaries and dashboards for executives. Finally, feedback is gathered from stakeholders to improve the intelligence process. This step helps identify shortcomings, adjust priorities, and enhance data collection methods, ensuring the program adapts to evolving requirements and remains effective over time [11]. Threat intelligence lifecycle stages are illustrated in Table 3.12.

Threat Intelligence Lifecycles are continuous and iterative processes that ensure organizations remain informed and prepared to deal with ever-changing threats.

3.6.7 Challenges in Cyber Security Intelligence

Cybersecurity intelligence faces several critical challenges that require focused strategies. Data overload and noise make it challenging to detect genuine threats amidst vast amounts of information. Attribution difficulties complicate efforts to trace the origins of attacks, especially as attackers use techniques to mask their identities. Balancing privacy with intelligence gathering introduces ethical concerns, particularly as monitoring efforts increase. Timeliness and relevance of intelligence are also crucial; outdated or irrelevant data can lead to ineffective responses [12]. In a nutshell, cybersecurity intelligence faces four primary challenges:

1. **Data Overload and Noise**: With vast amounts of data collected from multiple endpoints, irrelevant or low-value information often obscures real threats, making it difficult to filter out noise while retaining potential indicators. Extracting actionable insights without discarding valuable data is essential.

Table 3.12 Threat intelligence lifecycle

Stage	Description	Key activities	Output examples
Direction	Defines the goals and requirements of the threat intelligence program.	– Identifying threats to monitor. – Setting intelligence priorities. – Determining stakeholder needs.	Intelligence requirements, monitoring priorities, stakeholder-specific goals.
Collection	Gather raw data from various sources based on the defined requirements.	– Using automated tools. – Conducting manual research. – Leveraging human intelligence sources.	Logs, network traffic data, threat feeds, OSINT reports.
Processing	Cleans, structures, and formats raw data for analysis, integrating data from disparate sources.	– Filtering irrelevant information. – Normalizing and structuring data. – Preparing data for analysis.	Structured threat data, filtered indicators of compromise (IOCs).
Analysis	Evaluates processed data to extract meaningful insights about threats and vulnerabilities.	– Identifying threat actors. – Detecting attack patterns. – Assessing vulnerabilities.	Actionable intelligence, attack pattern reports, vulnerability assessments.
Dissemination	Shares analyzed intelligence with relevant stakeholders in an appropriate and timely format.	– Preparing reports, dashboards, and alerts. – Tailoring information to the audience (e.g., technical or executive-level).	SOC technical reports, executive summaries, intelligence alerts.
Feedback	Collects stakeholder feedback to refine and improve the intelligence lifecycle.	– Identifying intelligence gaps. – Adjusting priorities. Refining data collection strategies.	Revised intelligence priorities, updated collection and analysis strategies.

2. **Attribution Difficulties**: Identifying the origin or source of cyberattacks is complex, especially as sophisticated attackers use methods to obscure their activities. Effective attribution is critical for defensive strategies, yet it's frequently hindered by anonymity tactics and international jurisdiction issues.
3. **Balancing Privacy with Intelligence Gathering**: Intelligence collection must be balanced with privacy protection, particularly under stringent regulations. Organizations need to gather adequate threat data while ensuring user privacy and maintaining compliance with privacy laws.
4. **Timeliness and Relevance of Intelligence**: Cyber threat intelligence must be both timely and relevant to enable effective response. Detecting and responding to threats rapidly, before they escalate, is crucial in today's fast-evolving cyber landscape.

It should be noted that attackers are growing increasingly sophisticated, adapting faster than defenses can keep pace. Thus, to remain effective, cybersecurity intelligence must refine data processing, enhance source verification, uphold privacy standards, and ensure timely threat detection and response.

3.6.7.1 Federated Learning in Cybersecurity: Potential and Limitations

Federated learning methods offer powerful solutions that enhance cybersecurity intelligence by preserving privacy, filtering data for relevance, and addressing attribution challenges. By tackling these issues, federated learning improves the effectiveness of cybersecurity intelligence, enabling organizations to respect privacy standards while ensuring threat data remains relevant and actionable. This subsection classifies cybersecurity challenges into two categories: those that can be effectively addressed using federated learning and those that, by their nature, are not suited to federated learning as a solution [9–12].

3.6.7.1.1 Aspects of Federated Learning that Suit Cybersecurity Challenges

Federated learning effectively addresses several cybersecurity challenges by enhancing data privacy, improving real-time intelligence, and enabling collaborative threat detection without compromising sensitive information. Federated Learning aligns with key cybersecurity challenges as shown in Table 3.13.

By aligning with these aspects, Federated Learning enhances cybersecurity resilience, upholds privacy, and fosters collaboration.

3.6.7.1.2 Federated Learning Possible Solutions for Challenges in Cyber Security Intelligence

Federated learning helps address cybersecurity challenges by enhancing collaboration, preserving data privacy, and increasing the responsiveness of threat detection systems—each a critical element in a strong cybersecurity framework. Table 3.14 describes federated learning possible solutions for current challenges in Cybersecurity Intelligence.

3.6.7.1.3 Challenges that Are Not Naturally Suited to Federated Learning

Some challenges are inherently unsuited to federated learning due to its federated and modular structure, which introduces limitations in data heterogeneity, resource variability, communication, and privacy.

In federated learning, data remains on local devices, leading to heterogeneous data distributions across clients. This diversity can impact model convergence and

Table 3.13 Cyber security challenge and federated learning solution

The cyber security challenge	Federated learning solution	Key benefits	Use cases
Privacy and data security	FL processes data locally, ensuring sensitive information is not shared or transferred.	– Maintains data privacy and security. – Addresses legal and ethical concerns in data sharing.	User behavior analysis, financial fraud detection, healthcare cybersecurity.
Real-time threat detection and response	FL enables continuous model updates by aggregating insights from multiple data sources without accessing raw data.	– Ensures faster adaptation to new threats. – Improves timeliness and relevance of intelligence.	Detecting zero-day vulnerabilities, evolving malware detection.
Collaborative intelligence gathering	Supports indirect sharing of threat intelligence insights through model updates, bypassing data-sharing issues.	– Strengthens collective defenses. – Enables collaboration without compromising sensitive data.	Cross-organization threat intelligence sharing, such as in ISACs.
Enhanced attribution and attack analysis	Leverages distributed learning to identify context-specific threat patterns, improving detection and attribution.	– Provides broader threat context. – Enhances accuracy in identifying threat origins.	Analyzing phishing campaigns, tracing ransomware attack sources across industries.

Table 3.14 Challenge in cybersecurity intelligence and federated learning solution

Challenge in cybersecurity intelligence	Federated learning solution
Data overload and noise	Selective model aggregation: FL can aggregate only relevant insights from distributed sources, filtering out redundant or low-value information. This approach minimizes noise while enhancing model quality and relevance.
Attribution difficulties	Cross-entity collaborative modeling: FL allows multiple organizations to jointly train models on attack patterns without sharing raw data, improving attribution accuracy by leveraging diverse threat data while maintaining privacy.
Balancing privacy with intelligence gathering	Decentralized data processing: FL enables collaborative learning without transferring raw data, allowing organizations to gather intelligence insights while preserving individual data privacy, thus aligning with legal and ethical standards.
Timeliness and relevance of intelligence	Continuous, real-time model updates: FL facilitates continuous model updates across distributed sources, ensuring that cybersecurity models reflect the latest threat trends in real-time, enhancing response speed and accuracy.
Adapting to sophisticated, evolving threats	Personalized models for diverse environments: FL enables model personalization at each client location, allowing cybersecurity systems to adapt to the specific threat landscape of different organizations or regions, thereby improving defense against emerging threats.

accuracy, as each participant may have unique data characteristics. Additionally, federated learning relies on multiple devices, often with limited resources, which may lack the computational power or network bandwidth to support frequent model updates, resulting in inconsistent performance. The need for regular communication between devices and a central server also introduces latency and bandwidth issues, constraining scalability in large networks.

Privacy is another key concern. While federated learning avoids sharing raw data, the transmission of model updates can still expose local data insights, posing risks like model inversion attacks. Addressing these privacy risks without compromising model effectiveness requires advanced, often resource-intensive techniques.

These challenges arise from federated learning's fundamental structure, which emphasizes data privacy and decentralization but encounters obstacles in situations that require centralized processing, consistent data distributions, and robust client resources. Although federated learning is promising, certain challenges in cybersecurity and other areas are not well-suited to it. There are a few key challenges and potential solutions for diverse and resource-constrained environments, complex cybersecurity use cases that are shown in Table 3.15.

Table 3.15 Challenges that are not naturally suited to FL

Challenge	Why not naturally suited to FL	Possible solution
Heterogeneity of data	Data distribution and quality can vary greatly across participants, impacting model convergence and accuracy.	Personalized federated learning: Tailor models to each client's data, allowing local adaptations that account for specific patterns and variations in data.
Limited resources for small clients	Clients with limited computational power or bandwidth may struggle to participate fully in FL, impacting overall model performance.	Federated averaging with resource-aware scheduling: Adjust model updates to account for client resource constraints and prioritize updates from more capable devices.
Latency and communication overhead	Frequent communication between clients and the central server can cause delays, particularly in large, distributed networks.	Asynchronous FL or communication-efficient protocols: Use asynchronous updates or compressed data transmissions to reduce communication frequency and bandwidth usage.
Privacy risks with model updates	Although raw data isn't shared, model updates can still reveal patterns that could lead to privacy breaches (e.g., via model inversion attacks).	Differential privacy and secure aggregation: Apply differential privacy to model updates and use secure aggregation protocols to prevent inference attacks on model updates.
Difficulty in handling complex dependencies	Certain cybersecurity models require interdependent data from different sources, which FL's decentralized approach may struggle to capture.	Hybrid FL with centralized aggregation for key dependencies: Use FL for most processes while centrally aggregating specific complex dependencies only when essential, ensuring comprehensive intelligence without compromising privacy.

3.7 Summary

Chapter 3, Fundamentals of Cybersecurity, provides a foundational understanding of cybersecurity's critical aspects, highlighting the importance of protecting digital systems and data. As the chapter begins, it examines the Cybersecurity Landscape. Next, the chapter examines the Principles of Cybersecurity, which include confidentiality, integrity, availability, and other guiding concepts that shape effective security practices. These principles serve as the backbone for designing cyber-resistant systems. The section on Cybersecurity Key Concepts and Terminology introduces essential terms and frameworks that help comprehend the domain's complexities. This foundational knowledge is crucial for identifying vulnerabilities and developing effective countermeasures.

This chapter explores the diverse types of attacks, such as malware, phishing, and denial-of-service attacks, while highlighting their mechanisms and potential impact on organizations. Understanding these threats provides the basis for targeted defense strategies. Finally, the chapter concludes with Cyber Security Intelligence. It discusses the tools, processes, and strategies for gathering, analyzing, and utilizing intelligence to predict, prevent, and respond to cyber threats.

3.8 Conclusion

Throughout this chapter, the importance of a robust and proactive cybersecurity approach is underlined. Understanding the evolving threat landscape and applying foundational principles can help us defend against cyberattacks. This chapter presents insights that can help individuals and organizations adapt to the dynamic challenges of cybersecurity.

References

1. Verma, R. (2021). Cybersecurity and privacy fundamentals. In *The smart cyber ecosystem for sustainable development* (pp. 353–377).
2. Choo, K. K. R. (2011). The cyber threat landscape: Challenges and future research directions. *Computers & Security, 30*(8), 719–731.
3. Ramirez, R., & Choucri, N. (2016). Improving interdisciplinary communication with standardized cyber security terminology: a literature review. *IEEE Access, 4*, 2216–2243.
4. Wilson, K. S., & Kiy, M. A. (2014). Some fundamental cybersecurity concepts. *IEEE Access, 2*, 116–124.
5. Nespoli, P., Gomez Marmol, F., & Maestre Vidal, J. (2021). Battling against cyberattacks: Towards pre-standardization of countermeasures. *Cluster Computing, 24*, 57–81.
6. Li, Y., & Liu, Q. (2021). A comprehensive review study of cyber-attacks and cyber security; Emerging trends and recent developments. *Energy Reports, 7*, 8176–8186.

7. Bendovschi, A. (2015). Cyber-attacks–trends, patterns and security countermeasures. *Procedia Economics and Finance, 28*, 24–31.
8. Avdeeva, I., Golovina, T., Guzhina, G., Sulima, E., Suhanov, D., & Tihanov, E. (2021, March). The concept of preventive cybersecurity management of the IoT device market in the digital economy. In IV *International scientific and practical conference* (pp. 1–6).
9. Sarker, I. H., Furhad, M. H., & Nowrozy, R. (2021). Ai-driven cybersecurity: An overview, security intelligence modeling and research directions. *SN Computer Science, 2*(3), 173.
10. Li, J. H. (2018). Cyber security meets artificial intelligence: A survey. *Frontiers of Information Technology & Electronic Engineering, 19*(12), 1462–1474.
11. Möller, D. P. (2023). Threats and threat intelligence. In *Guide to cybersecurity in digital transformation: Trends, methods, technologies, applications and best practices* (pp. 71–129). Springer Nature Switzerland.
12. Zhang, Z., Ning, H., Shi, F., Farha, F., Xu, Y., Xu, J., et al. (2022). Artificial intelligence in cyber security: Research advances, challenges, and opportunities. *Artificial Intelligence Review*, 1–25.

Chapter 4
Cyber Security Intelligent Systems Based on Federated Learning

4.1 Introduction

Analysing cybersecurity data using traditional machine learning models poses data privacy and security hazards. Federated Learning, as discussed in previous chapters, is capable of creating a system in which multiple parties or clients can share insights about their local data without compromising privacy. The integration of machine learning (ML) into cyber security has led to significant advancements, enabling more sophisticated detection and response mechanisms. FL emerges as a promising paradigm, offering a decentralised approach where multiple clients collaboratively train a shared model while keeping their data local. This chapter delves into the limitations of traditional ML in cyber security and explores various cyber security systems that leverage the advantages of FL. In the following the key reasons behind these limitations has been discussed.

4.1.1 Data Privacy and Security

Data-driven methods have revolutionised the way data is processed. However, this data-hungry approach faces growing concerns over data privacy [1]. Data breaches and unauthorised access to central repositories as centralised ML models require, can compromise sensitive information, posing a substantial risk to individuals and organisations.

Privacy Risks: traditional ML models require collecting and storing vast amounts of data from different sources in a central location. This central repository becomes a prime target for cyber attacks, which could lead to the exposure of sensitive information, including personal data and proprietary business information [2].

© The Author(s), under exclusive license to Springer Nature Switzerland AG 2025
H. Tabrizchi, A. Aghasi, *Federated Cyber Intelligence*, SpringerBriefs in Computer Science, https://doi.org/10.1007/978-3-031-86592-3_4

Compliance Issues: Many industries are subject to stringent data protection regulations such as general data protection regulation (GDPR), the health insurance portability and accountability act (HIPAA), and the california consumer privacy act (CCPA). Centralised data collection can complicate compliance with these regulations, leading to legal and financial repercussions for organisations [3].

4.1.2   Scalability Issues

Traditional ML systems often struggle with scalability, especially in the context of large and diverse datasets typical in cyber security applications. Centralized data processing can become a bottleneck, limiting the ability to scale solutions efficiently across different environments and infrastructures.

Resource Intensive: As the volume of data grows, the computational and storage resources required to process and analyse this data in a centralized manner also increase exponentially. This can lead to significant infrastructure costs and processing delays [4].

Latency: Real-time threat detection requires rapid data processing and analysis. Centralized systems can suffer from latency issues due to the need to transfer large datasets over the network, which can delay threat detection and response times [5].

4.1.3   Data Heterogeneity

Cyber security data comes in various forms, such as network logs, user activity records, and threat intelligence feeds. Traditional ML approaches may struggle to integrate and process these heterogeneous data types effectively, resulting in suboptimal performance of security systems.

On the other hand, Cyber security involves a wide range of data types, including structured data such as logs, unstructured data like emails, and semi-structured data including JSON files. Integrating these diverse data types into a single model can be challenging for traditional ML approaches.

Other primary tasks that need to be done are normalization and preprocessing. Each type of data may require different preprocessing steps, normalization techniques, and feature extraction methods. Centralized systems must account for these variations, adding complexity to the data processing pipeline.

4.1.4   Continuous Learning and Adaptation

Cyber threats are constantly evolving, requiring ML models to be regularly updated with new data to maintain their effectiveness. Traditional ML models deployed in a centralized manner often face delays in updates, leading to periods of vulnerability where the models may not effectively detect new threats.

Update Delays: Centralized ML models typically undergo periodic updates, which can be slow and infrequent. During the intervals between updates, new types of threats may emerge that the model is not equipped to handle.

Resource Constraints: Updating a centralized model involves significant computational resources and can disrupt the normal operation of the system. Organizations may delay updates to avoid these disruptions, further exacerbating the problem.

4.2 Federated Learning in Cyber Security Systems

Addressing the growing need for collaboration in detecting and mitigating complex cyber threats while preserving data privacy, FL can play a significant role in cyber security defense mechanisms. As said before, Traditional cybersecurity approaches often rely on centralized machine learning models trained on aggregated data, which creates significant privacy risks and compliance challenges, especially in sensitive industries like finance, healthcare, and government. FL redefines this model by enabling decentralized training across distributed data sources, ensuring that sensitive information remains local while contributing to a global model. This approach is particularly suited to cybersecurity, where threat intelligence is often fragmented across organizations, and real-time, privacy-conscious collaboration is critical for staying ahead of evolving threats.

The integration of FL into cybersecurity systems unlocks new possibilities for threat detection, anomaly identification, and predictive analytics. It allows organizations to leverage collective intelligence to identify emerging attack patterns, such as phishing campaigns or malware variants, without exposing proprietary or sensitive data. By uniting decentralized data sources and expertise across industries, FL fosters robust defense mechanisms that are both adaptive and scalable. Moreover, the ability to train models across diverse environments ensures that FL-based cybersecurity systems remain effective against a wide spectrum of attacks, from localized threats targeting specific sectors to global campaigns orchestrated by advanced persistent threat (APT) actors. In this section we deep dive into characterization of basic cyber security systems empowered by FL.

4.2.1 Federated Learning for Intrusion Detection Systems (IDS)

Intrusion Detection Systems are critical components of modern cybersecurity, designed to monitor network traffic and system activities to identify suspicious behavior and potential breaches. Traditional IDS approaches often rely on centralized data analysis, which can lead to delayed responses and privacy concerns, especially when handling sensitive organizational data. FL offers an interesting solution by enabling IDS to collaboratively train models across distributed networks without aggregating sensitive data in a central repository. This decentralized approach ensures that insights from diverse environments—such as corporate networks, IoT systems, and cloud infrastructures—are effectively utilized to enhance intrusion detection capabilities. By combining the strengths of distributed data and privacy-preserving machine learning, FL-based IDS systems can adapt to emerging threats in real time, maintain compliance with stringent data privacy regulations, and improve overall detection accuracy in complex and dynamic network environments.

4.2.1.1   Overview

An IDS is part of a cyber defence system that tries to detect network traffic which are suspected to be intrusive. They use some predetermined indicators, rules or inferred insights to classify network traffic packets into healthy and malicious categories [6]. Basically, IDS types can be divided into two categories:

Signature-based IDS: these systems analyse the network traffic, looking for signs of any threat or malicious activity by means of predefined signatures of known threats [7]. Signatures are unique patterns associated with known threats. These patterns can be strings of bytes, specific sequences of instructions, or any other identifiable data. The process starts with traffic analysing then it is tested against different signatures for pattern matching.

The process is illustrated in Fig. 4.1. Traffic segmenter decomposes the incoming traffic according to the signature structure. Signatures basically designed considering known attacks patterns. Thus signature-based IDSs have been vulnerable to zero-day attacks [8].

Fig. 4.1 Signature stack in a traditional IDS

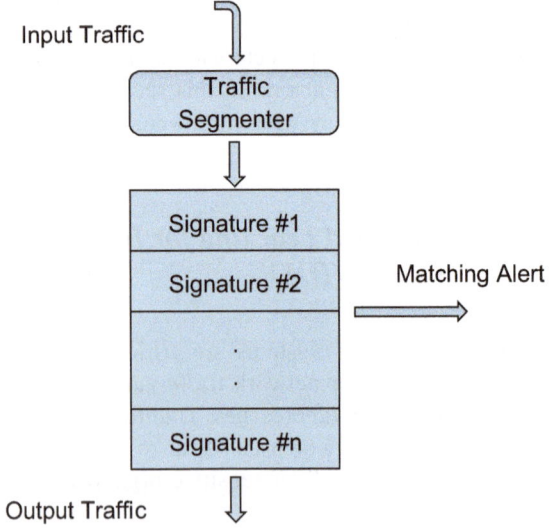

Because of their reliance on predetermined and well-defined samples, they can achieve a high level of accuracy and low false positive rate. The deployment of such a system is easy, but it requires frequent updates to cope with new threats. As the stack of signatures grows, the system's speed could be affected. Modern persistent threats urge the need for sophisticated methods that can inspect the threats behaviorally and are capable of detecting anomalies of incoming traffic. Such techniques rely on artificial intelligence concepts in general and focus on machine learning methods in particular. Therefore the main research direction of IDS development has been focused on adopting different machine learning methods [9]. Using historical data, ML methods can classify and predict incoming events and strengthen the decision making process by extracting meaningful insights without being explicitly programmed.

4.2.1.2   Implementation

Any ML-based system needs data for the model to be trained on. A stand alone IDS system relying on its own data samples gathered through its past operations not knowing what may happen on other systems may raise the risk of being compromised by attacks other organisations faced before. A wiser option is involving a more comprehensive model training on data from various endpoints and using. As we know from previous chapters, these systems can generally be implemented either based on a central repository where all the data piled up in a central repository or based on a more sophisticated approach called federated learning. Figure 4.2 shows an illustration of the first scenario that is grounded on a central learning of traffic patterns from distributed traffic sources. Despite the benefits, network data often includes sensitive information that can expose risks, such as user browsing histories, the applications they interact with, and vital endpoint information like domain controllers and firewalls. As a result, implementing a centralized learning approach can introduce significant privacy, security, and transactional vulnerabilities that organizations typically aim to mitigate or prevent. Such risks could lead to potential breaches of confidentiality and integrity, prompting many organizations to reconsider or avoid centralized data management strategies altogether [6].

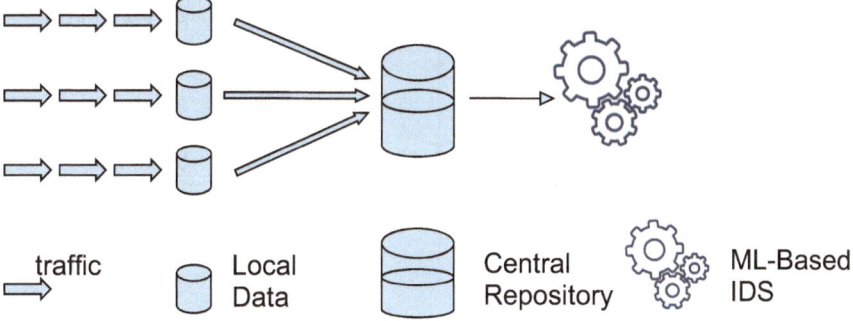

Fig. 4.2 Centralized ML IDS

In a federated IDS, each node or endpoint like a company's network trains a local model on its own data. Periodically, these local models are aggregated to form a global model that benefits from the collective knowledge of all nodes. This approach maintains data privacy and leverages diverse datasets to improve detection accuracy. The concept is depicted in Fig. 4.3.

4.2.1.3 Benefits

Privacy Preservation: Local data never leaves the node, reducing the risk of data breaches. This ensures compliance with privacy regulations and minimizes the risk of sensitive data exposure.

Improved Detection: The global model benefits from diverse datasets, enhancing its ability to detect a wide range of threats. By incorporating data from multiple sources, the model can identify patterns and anomalies that may not be apparent in a single dataset.

Scalability: The decentralized nature of FL allows IDS to scale across multiple nodes efficiently. Each node processes its own data, reducing the computational burden on central servers and enabling real-time analysis.

4.2.2   Federated Learning for Malware Detection

Malware detection systems play a vital role in safeguarding digital infrastructure by identifying and mitigating malicious software that can compromise systems and data. Traditional malware detection methods often rely on centralized machine learning models, which require the collection and aggregation of malware samples from various sources. This approach raises significant privacy concerns and may

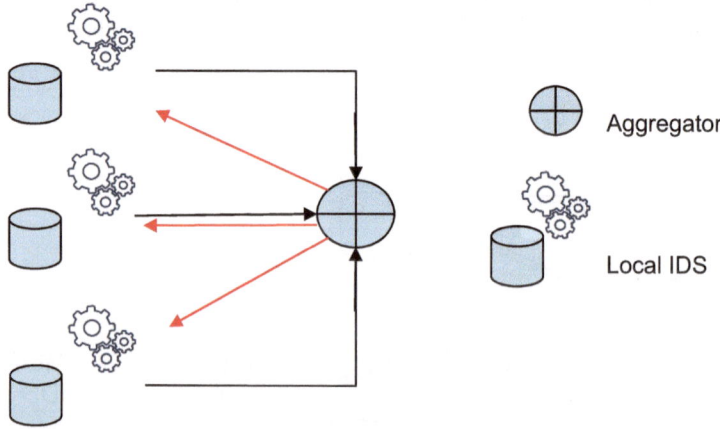

Fig. 4.3 General architecture of an FL based IDs

limit the diversity of data used for training, reducing the model's ability to detect novel or advanced malware. FL addresses these challenges by enabling decentralized collaboration among organizations to train malware detection models without sharing sensitive data. Through FL, diverse malware datasets from different environments—such as enterprise systems, cloud platforms, and IoT devices—can collectively contribute to a robust and adaptive global model [10]. This approach not only enhances the detection of emerging malware variants but also ensures compliance with data protection regulations, fostering a secure and privacy-preserving framework for malware defense.

4.2.2.1 Overview

Before the adoption of ML techniques, traditional malware detection relied primarily on signature-based and heuristic methods. Signature-based detection involves identifying malware by comparing code against a database of known malware signatures—unique strings of data or code patterns associated with malicious software [11]. These methods, while effective for known threats, have several significant limitations. The primary drawback is their inability to detect new or evolving malware, often called zero-day threats, which lack an existing signature. Signature-based systems require regular updates to their databases to keep up with the rapidly evolving threat landscape, leading to periods where newly discovered malware can evade detection.

To improve upon this, heuristic-based methods were developed, which attempt to identify malware based on its behavior rather than a specific signature. These systems monitor files and programs for suspicious activity, such as attempts to modify core system files or initiate unauthorized network connections [11]. However, heuristic methods can be prone to false positives, where benign software is incorrectly flagged as malicious. This creates a trade-off between sensitivity and accuracy, as highly sensitive systems may generate too many alerts, while more conservative systems risk missing actual threats [12].

While both signature and heuristic-based approaches laid the foundation for malware detection, they struggled with scalability, adaptability, and the increasing complexity of modern malware. The rapid evolution of malware strains, the sheer volume of data to analyze, and the need for real-time protection highlighted the limitations of these traditional methods. The growing sophistication of malware, including polymorphic malware that can modify its code to evade detection, created a pressing need for more intelligent, adaptable solutions.

4.2.2.2 Machine Learning for Malware Detection: Motivation and Challenges

The emergence of machine learning provided a promising new avenue for malware detection. ML algorithms can automatically learn patterns from vast datasets, enabling systems to detect previously unseen malware by identifying malicious behaviors, data patterns, or anomalies without relying on predefined signatures. This allows ML models to generalize and detect zero-day threats, making them more versatile than traditional methods. Additionally, machine learning can analyze vast amounts of data quickly, providing scalable solutions capable of handling the enormous datasets that modern cyber security systems must process.

Machine learning-based malware detection systems are typically trained on historical data, where labeled datasets of malware and benign software are used to teach the model to distinguish between malicious and non-malicious behavior. These models can analyze various features, such as file structure, execution behavior, network traffic patterns, and system calls, enabling more accurate and comprehensive detection [13].

However, despite the advantages, traditional machine learning models also face several challenges that limit their effectiveness. One of the most pressing challenges is data privacy. To train an effective ML model, a vast amount of data from various devices and environments is required, often involving sensitive or proprietary information. This raises privacy concerns, particularly in industries such as healthcare and finance, where data protection regulations are stringent. Centralizing all this data in one location for model training makes it vulnerable to breaches or misuse, which is a significant drawback.

Another challenge is scalability. As the volume of data continues to grow, centralized machine learning models become difficult to manage. Collecting, storing, and processing large datasets from multiple devices requires significant computational resources and infrastructure. Furthermore, transferring data from individual devices to a central server introduces latency, which is particularly problematic in systems that require real-time detection, such as malware detection on edge or IoT devices [14].

A further limitation is adaptability. Cyber threats evolve rapidly, and malware is becoming increasingly sophisticated. Traditional machine learning models often struggle to keep up with these evolving threats because they require periodic retraining and updating. This process can be slow and resource-intensive, leaving systems vulnerable to new forms of malware during the intervals between updates. Furthermore, the central model may not be able to incorporate local-specific threats that individual devices or environments encounter, making it less effective in certain contexts.

These challenges create a strong motivation for the adoption of federated learning in malware detection systems. Federated learning offers a decentralized approach that addresses the privacy, scalability, and adaptability issues associated with traditional ML-based solutions. Instead of sending all data to a central server for training, FL enables individual devices to train local models using their own data. The insights from these local models are then aggregated to form a global model, without any raw data ever leaving the device. This approach preserves data privacy, reduces the need for massive data transfers, and allows for more frequent updates to the global model, ensuring that it remains adaptable to new malware threats.

Federated learning, therefore, offers a balanced solution to the limitations of traditional malware detection methods, providing the scalability, real-time adaptability, and privacy protection that modern cyber security systems require.

4.2.2.3   Implementation

Implementing a federated learning based malware detection system involves several key steps, processes, and considerations to ensure the system is both effective in detecting malware and efficient in preserving privacy. This section delves into the implementation of such a system, using detailed examples and simulated data to illustrate how federated learning can improve malware detection.

4.2.2.3.1   Architecture of Federated Learning-Based Malware Detection

At a high level, a federated learning malware detection system consists of several devices (clients), such as personal computers, smartphones, or IoT devices, which each train a local model on their data. These devices communicate with a central server, which aggregates the locally trained models into a global model. The key feature of this system is that no raw data leaves the devices, preserving privacy while still leveraging the collective intelligence from a wide range of environments.

Each device collects and labels data on detected malware or malicious behaviour. These data points could include information on suspicious file behaviours, unusual network traffic, or deviations in software execution patterns. Once a sufficient amount of local data has been accumulated, the device trains a local machine learning model, which learns to identify malware based on the features present in the data.

To better understand how federated learning is applied, consider a scenario with multiple organisations—each of which runs their own fleet of devices and computers that may encounter different types of malware.

Step 1: Local Data Collection and Preprocessing

Each organization's devices gather local data, such as logs from network traffic, file execution metadata, and system behavior patterns. For example, in one organization, devices might detect a spike in traffic to certain suspicious IP addresses, which suggests potential malware communications. In another organization, devices might record unusual system file modifications or execution of untrusted code, hinting at ransomware or trojans. Each device preprocesses this data locally, extracting features such as file hash values, application programming interface (API) calls, memory usage, and I/O behavior, creating a dataset labeled with malware or benign labels (Table 4.1).

Step 2: Local Model Training

Each device trains a local machine learning model, such as a random forest or neural network, on this preprocessed data. These local models learn to identify patterns in the features that correspond to malware activity. For instance, a model might learn that frequent access to certain API calls combined with communication to suspicious IP addresses often correlates with ransomware.

At this stage, only the models are trained on the device—no raw data is shared with external entities. This ensures that sensitive information, such as network logs or specific file behaviours, remains private to the organisation.

Step 3: Federated Aggregation of Local Models

After training, each device sends its locally trained model to a central server. Importantly, this does not involve sending the underlying data, only the model parameters (such as the weights of a neural network). The central server aggregates these local models to create a global model, using techniques like Federated Averaging. This global model benefits from the knowledge gained across all devices, without ever accessing the raw data from any of them.

For example, the global model might combine knowledge of file behaviours indicative of malware from one organization with suspicious network patterns from another, allowing it to detect a broader range of threats than any individual device's local model could (Table 4.2).

Step 4: Model Updates and Deployment

The aggregated global model is sent back to each participating device, where it is deployed for real-time malware detection. Each device now benefits from a model trained on data from across the network, enhancing its ability to detect malware that

Table 4.1 Example of a Program Behaviour Log

Feature	Description	Example Value
File hash	Unique hash of the file	efgh5678abcd1234
Memory usage	Amount of memory used by the process	256 MB
API calls	Specific API calls made by malware	NtCreateFile
Execution time	Time taken to execute the program	2.5 sec
Network IPs	IP addresses contacted by program	192.168.0.101

Table 4.2 Aggregation of Local model with weight of contribution

Organization	Local model accuracy	Contribution to global model
Org A	92%	High weight
Org B	88%	Medium weight
Org C	90%	High weight

may not have appeared in its local environment but was encountered by other devices.

For example, if Org A's environment saw new strains of spyware, and Org C experienced an influx of ransomware variants, the global model would now be capable of detecting both types across all participating devices.

4.2.2.3.2 Performance Metrics

Evaluating the effectiveness of FL-based malware detection systems requires robust performance metrics that reflect the system's ability to accurately identify threats while addressing unique challenges such as data heterogeneity and resource constraints. Key metrics for assessing these systems include detection accuracy, precision, recall, F1-score, communication overhead, and convergence time, all of which provide insight into both the technical performance and practical feasibility of the approach.

Detection accuracy measures the proportion of correctly identified samples, both benign and malicious, and serves as a baseline for evaluating the model's reliability. Precision and recall offer deeper insights into detection quality, where precision assesses the proportion of true positives among all positive predictions, and recall measures the proportion of true positives detected among all actual malicious samples. For example, a system deployed across various organizations may yield high recall in detecting malware but low precision if it misidentifies legitimate software as malicious, leading to false alarms. The F1-score balances precision and recall, offering a single metric for overall detection performance, which is particularly important when malware datasets are imbalanced, as malicious samples often constitute a minority of total data.

FL-based systems introduce additional considerations such as communication overhead and convergence time, which measure the cost of distributed training and the time taken for the global model to stabilize, respectively. Communication overhead quantifies the bandwidth required to exchange model updates between participating devices, a critical factor in resource-constrained environments like IoT ecosystems or mobile networks. Convergence time assesses how quickly the system can adapt to new malware threats, which is crucial for real-time applications. For instance, in an FL-based malware detection system deployed across edge devices, rapid convergence ensures timely updates to counter emerging malware variants while minimizing interruptions to normal operations.

Furthermore, the diversity and distribution of data in FL settings require evaluating the robustness of the model to non-iid data, as malware samples may vary significantly across devices or regions. A robust system should maintain high performance even when training data is not evenly distributed or follows different patterns. Similarly, privacy preservation metrics assess the system's ability to protect sensitive data during the training process, ensuring compliance with regulations like GDPR and avoiding leakage of proprietary information. By combining traditional performance metrics with FL-specific considerations, such as communication efficiency and robustness to heterogeneity, malware detection systems can be rigorously evaluated to ensure they meet the demands of modern cybersecurity challenges. These metrics not only gauge technical performance but also determine the practicality of deploying FL-based solutions across diverse environments, from enterprise networks to IoT ecosystems.

4.2.2.3.3   Example Use Case: Federated Malware Detection in IoT Networks

Consider an IoT-based smart home network, where each device—such as smart TVs, refrigerators, and home security systems—can be compromised by malware targeting vulnerabilities specific to IoT systems. In a traditional centralized system, data from each device would need to be sent to a cloud server for analysis, which introduces privacy concerns and increases latency (Fig. 4.4).

Using federated learning, each IoT device can train its own local model to detect potential malware based on its unique activity patterns for instance consider unusual traffic from a smart thermostat. These local models are then aggregated at the edge or cloud level, creating a global model capable of detecting malware across all connected devices without compromising user privacy. If a new malware strain affecting smart refrigerators is detected in one household, the global model can learn from that example and prevent similar attacks across all smart homes in the network.

4.2.2.4   Benefits

Enhanced Privacy: User data remains on their devices, protecting sensitive information. This decentralized approach ensures that personal and proprietary data is not exposed to potential security risks.

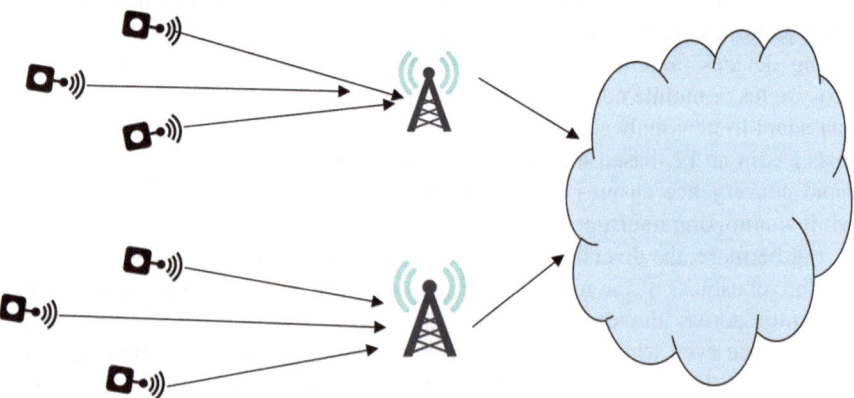

Fig. 4.4 Example configuration use case

Adaptability: Continuous local training ensures models are up-to-date with the latest malware variants. As new malware is detected on individual devices, the local models adapt and improve, which then contributes to the global model.

Resource Efficiency: Distributed training reduces the computational load on centralized servers. Each device only needs to process its own data, which can lead to more efficient use of resources and faster model updates.

4.2.3   Federated Learning for Phishing Detection

Phishing remains one of the most common and damaging types of cyberattacks, where attackers trick individuals into revealing sensitive information, such as passwords, financial details, or personal data, by posing as legitimate entities. Phishing detection systems aim to identify and mitigate such threats through a combination of rule-based, heuristic, and machine learning techniques. Federated learning introduces a privacy-preserving, scalable, and adaptive approach to enhance phishing detection, addressing the limitations of traditional methods.

4.2.3.1   Overview

Before machine learning, phishing detection relied on rule-based systems that scanned emails or web pages for suspicious keywords, URLs, or metadata. While these systems were effective in identifying known phishing patterns, they struggled with novel, sophisticated attacks that used obfuscation techniques or evolved over time. For example, attackers could bypass such systems by subtly altering the spelling of words, using visually similar domain names, or embedding malicious links in QR codes [15].

Machine learning offered a significant advancement by analyzing features extracted from emails, web pages, and URLs to identify phishing attempts. Features such as domain age, URL length, email headers, and hyperlink behavior were used to train models capable of detecting previously unseen phishing attacks. However, ML-based phishing detection systems faced several challenges:

1. **Privacy Concerns**: Training ML models required collecting vast amounts of user data, including sensitive emails, URLs, and browsing behavior, raising significant privacy concerns.
2. **Adaptability**: Centralized models struggled to quickly adapt to new phishing tactics, as they relied on periodic retraining with updated datasets.
3. **Scalability**: Transferring large amounts of data from distributed devices to a central server for training incurred high communication costs and latency, making real-time detection challenging.

Federated Learning addresses these issues by enabling decentralized training of phishing detection models, allowing devices to collaboratively improve detection capabilities without sharing raw data.

4.2.3.2 Architecture and Implementation

Federated Learning can be applied to phishing detection by enabling email clients or web browsers to train local models on their user interactions. These local models are then aggregated to improve the global phishing detection model. Let delves into it by bringing an example:

Consider a scenario involving multiple organizations or individual users who encounter phishing attempts in different forms:

4.2.3.2.1 Step 1: Local Data Collection and Preprocessing

Each device collects phishing-related data from emails, URLs, and web traffic. For instance, an email client may identify suspicious messages using indicators such as mismatched sender domains or requests for sensitive information. A browser might detect phishing websites based on unusual domain behavior, such as recently registered domains or excessive redirects.

Preprocessing extracts features from this data to build a dataset for training. Examples of features include (Table 4.3):

For example, a suspicious email might contain the sender domain m1crosoft-support.com (a spoof of Microsoft) and an embedded link leading to a newly registered domain with several redirects.

4.2.3.2.2 Step 2: Local Model Training

Each device trains a phishing detection model on its local dataset. For example, a machine learning model like a gradient boosting classifier or a neural network might analyze features to determine whether an email or URL is phishing or legitimate. A model trained locally on a single device might learn that certain keyword patterns or domain characteristics correlate with phishing attempts.

Table 4.3 Phishing local data

Feature	Description	Example value
Domain age	Age of the domain in days	5 days
URL length	Total character count of the URL	120
HTTPS usage	Whether the site uses HTTPS	No
Keyword presence	Keywords like "login" or "verify" in the URL	Yes
Redirection count	Number of times the URL redirects	3
Sender email domain	Domain in the sender's email address	example.com

4.2.3.2.3   Step 3: Federated Aggregation of Local Models

Once the local training is complete, each device sends its model parameters such as weights for a neural network to a central server. These parameters, rather than raw data, are aggregated using methods like Federated Averaging to create a global model.

The global model benefits from diverse data across all devices. For instance, one user's local model might have learned to identify spear-phishing attacks targeting executives, while another user's model might specialize in identifying phishing websites related to financial scams. Aggregating these models enables the global model to detect a wider variety of phishing (Table 4.4).

4.2.3.2.4   Step 4: Model Updates and Deployment

Phishing threats in the context of smart cities present a unique and complex challenge. Smart cities rely heavily on interconnected systems, such as smart grids, intelligent traffic management, and IoT-based public utilities. Attackers can exploit these systems using phishing attacks to compromise email accounts, social engineering attacks on utility operators, or malicious links targeting public kiosks or smart devices. A federated learning-based phishing detection system can play a pivotal role in safeguarding these critical infrastructures without breaching the privacy of citizens or operators.

Imagine a smart city where various public and private entities—including municipal offices, hospitals, traffic systems, and utility providers—regularly exchange data. Each entity uses its devices and systems, which are vulnerable to phishing attacks tailored to their specific context. A centralized phishing detection system would require collecting sensitive data from all these entities, creating significant privacy and trust concerns. Federated learning, however, allows each entity to train a phishing detection model on its own environment while contributing to a global, privacy-preserving model.

4.2.3.2.5   Implementation Steps in Smart City Context

Step 1. Local Model Training by Each Entity
Each organization in the smart city trains a phishing detection model based on its specific environment. For instance:

Table 4.4 Aggregation of local phishing data

Device/user	Local model accuracy	Contribution to global model
User A (Corporate)	90%	High weight
User B (Home user)	85%	Medium weight
User C (IoT device)	88%	Medium weight

- **Municipal offices** analyze phishing attempts targeting administrative emails with fake tax refund claims.
- **Hospitals** focus on phishing links embedded in fraudulent patient records or appointment requests.
- **Smart traffic systems** detect phishing attempts that target operators with fake emergency alerts or update requests.

Example features extracted for phishing detection in a smart city environment might include (Table 4.5):

Step 2. Federated Aggregation for Global Model
The trained models from various entities are sent as encrypted parameter updates to the central server, which aggregates them to form a global phishing detection model. This global model benefits from diverse phishing attack patterns across different city sectors. For example, the system learns to detect a broad spectrum of phishing strategies, from spear-phishing targeting city officials to automated phishing campaigns targeting public utility users.

Step 3. Global Model Deployment Back to Entities
The improved global model is redistributed to all participating devices and systems. The municipal offices can now better detect phishing attacks that share characteristics with those targeting hospitals or traffic systems, and vice versa.

4.2.3.3   Performance Metrics

When evaluating the performance of federated learning for phishing detection, several metrics are essential to determine the effectiveness, efficiency, privacy, and adaptability of the system in distributed environments. These metrics provide insight into how FL compares to traditional machine learning approaches and how well it addresses challenges in real-world scenarios.

One fundamental metric is detection accuracy, which measures the proportion of phishing attempts and legitimate activities correctly identified by the system. High accuracy ensures the system reliably distinguishes phishing from legitimate communication. For example, in a test dataset of 1000 emails containing 300 phishing attempts, if the model identifies 280 phishing emails and 650 legitimate ones correctly, the accuracy would be 93%. In FL systems, accuracy may vary depending on the quality and diversity of the data distributed across local nodes. Unequal or

Table 4.5 Related feature extracted for phishing detection in smart city nodes

Feature	Description	Example value
Sender domain authenticity	Checks if the sender domain matches known entities	No
Embedded link behavior	Analyzes redirections and final destination behavior	Multiple redirects
Contextual relevance	Matches content with expected city operations	Low

biased data distributions can sometimes lead to reduced accuracy compared to centralized systems.

Another critical metric is precision, which evaluates the proportion of correctly flagged phishing attempts among all flagged instances. This metric is essential for minimizing false alarms, which are particularly problematic in phishing detection systems, as they may undermine user trust and lead to unnecessary interventions. For instance, if the system flags 320 emails as phishing but only 280 are actual phishing attempts, the precision would be 87.5%. The precision of FL models depends significantly on how local models contribute to the global model. Clients with noisy or low-quality data can introduce false patterns, which can reduce the precision unless robust aggregation techniques are applied.

Recall, or sensitivity, measures the system's ability to correctly identify actual phishing attempts. High recall is vital to ensure that phishing attacks are not overlooked, thereby reducing the risk of undetected threats. If, in a dataset with 300 phishing emails, the system detects 280 correctly but misses 20, the recall would be 93.3%. In FL, recall is influenced by the diversity of training data across nodes. FL systems trained on datasets with varying phishing patterns are more likely to generalize effectively, maintaining a high recall rate.

False positive rate (FPR) is another important metric, representing the proportion of legitimate cases incorrectly flagged as phishing. A low FPR minimizes disruptions to users by reducing the frequency of false alarms. For example, in a scenario with 700 legitimate emails, if 40 are wrongly flagged as phishing, the FPR would be 5.7%. FPR can be challenging to optimize in FL systems due to the potential for localized patterns in client data to skew global predictions. However, techniques such as differential privacy and regularization can help mitigate this issue.

Communication overhead is a unique concern for FL systems, representing the amount of data exchanged between local nodes and the central server during training. Efficient communication is crucial for scalability, particularly in environments with constrained network resources. For instance, if each client sends a 10 MB model update during 100 training rounds with 50 clients, the total communication cost would be 50GB. FL systems often use methods like model compression or selective communication to reduce these overheads without compromising performance.

Adaptation time, or the time taken to detect and adapt to new phishing patterns, is another critical metric. FL systems need to quickly integrate new threats into the global model to stay ahead of evolving phishing strategies. For example, if a novel phishing attack is introduced, an FL system may update the global model within 6 h compared to 24 h for a centralized system, demonstrating its ability to leverage parallel training and local updates for faster adaptation.

Privacy preservation is a cornerstone of FL-based phishing detection, assessing how well sensitive data remains secure during training and inference. Privacy metrics may involve measuring data leakage risks or evaluating the effectiveness of differential privacy mechanisms. For instance, a differential privacy implementation with a noise budget of $\varepsilon = 1$ can provide strong privacy guarantees while maintaining model utility. FL systems inherently reduce privacy risks by keeping data localized, but robust encryption and secure aggregation techniques further enhance this aspect.

Finally, scalability measures the system's ability to handle an increasing number of clients or data sources without significant performance degradation. Scalability is especially critical for phishing detection in distributed environments like smart cities or global networks. Metrics such as model convergence time and performance consistency across large-scale deployments are key indicators of scalability. For example, an FL system maintaining 90% accuracy across 10,000 IoT nodes demonstrates greater scalability than a centralized ML system that experiences significant accuracy loss due to bottlenecks in data aggregation.

These performance metrics, collectively, provide a comprehensive understanding of FL's potential in phishing detection. They highlight not only the technical capabilities of FL systems but also the trade-offs and advantages they offer over traditional approaches. Validating these metrics in real-world deployments or simulations, particularly in diverse and distributed environments, is crucial to fully realize the promise of FL for phishing detection.

4.2.3.4   PhishTank Dataset

The **PhishTank dataset** is a widely used resource in the field of phishing detection. It is maintained by the OpenDNS community, which collects, verifies, and shares information on suspected phishing URLs. PhishTank serves as a collaborative anti-phishing platform where users submit phishing URLs, which are then verified through crowdsourced validation. The dataset is freely available and extensively used in both research and industry for developing, benchmarking, and evaluating phishing detection systems [16].

4.2.3.4.1   Key Features and Applications

Its dynamic nature ensures that it stays updated with the latest phishing trends, providing real-time data on active phishing campaigns. This feature is particularly useful for systems designed to address current and emerging phishing threats. The dataset includes a wide variety of phishing URLs, targeting different sectors such as banking, social media, and e-commerce platforms. This diversity enhances its utility for training models that must generalize across a broad spectrum of phishing techniques.

A unique aspect of PhishTank is its reliance on community verification. Each URL submitted to the platform undergoes validation by community members, ensuring the authenticity of the data and reducing the likelihood of false positives. Furthermore, PhishTank is highly accessible. It offers an open API and downloadable data, enabling seamless integration into security systems and research workflows. This accessibility makes it a go-to resource for both academic and industrial applications.

The PhishTank dataset serves multiple applications. It is extensively used to train machine learning models by providing labeled data, enabling systems to distinguish between phishing and legitimate URLs. For instance, features such as URL length, subdomain count, and domain reputation are often extracted from the dataset and used as inputs to classifiers. Additionally, it is frequently employed to evaluate the performance of phishing detection systems, with metrics like accuracy, precision, and recall being assessed using the dataset. In real-world deployments, threat intelligence platforms integrate PhishTank data to enhance their ability to block malicious URLs, thereby protecting users from phishing attempts.

Another advanced application involves its use in federated learning settings. Researchers simulate distributed environments using subsets of the PhishTank dataset to evaluate the effectiveness of federated phishing detection systems. This approach allows them to assess how well FL systems can generalize and adapt to new threats without requiring centralized data collection.

Overall, the PhishTank dataset is indispensable for developing, testing, and deploying phishing detection technologies. It not only enables the creation of robust machine learning models but also supports real-time threat mitigation and innovative research in decentralized systems like federated learning.

4.2.3.4.2   Example Usage in Phishing Detection

Consider a machine learning-based phishing detection system. Features such as the domain age, presence of HTTPS, unusual characters, and URL length are extracted from each URL in the PhishTank dataset. These features are then used to train a model to classify URLs. For instance, URLs like http://login-secure-banking.com may appear legitimate but can be identified as phishing based on extracted patterns.

Here is an example table illustrating typical entries in the PhishTank dataset (Table 4.6):

Limitations of this dataset is listed in the following table

Bias toward verified URLs
Since the dataset relies on community verification, it might exclude some phishing URLs that are difficult to verify, potentially leading to sampling bias.

Short-lived URLs
Phishing URLs often have a short lifespan. By the time they are verified and included in the dataset, they may no longer be active, which could limit their relevance for real-time detection.

Lack of contextual information
The dataset primarily includes URLs without additional context, such as the phishing email's content or the website's structure. This limits its use for comprehensive phishing detection approaches that rely on more than URL features.

Table 4.6 Typical entries in the PhishTank dataset

Phishing URL	Target	Submission date	Verification status
http://secure-login-paypal.com	PayPal	10/1/2024	Verified
http://update-facebook-security.net	Facebook	10/2/2024	Verified
http://amazon-login.auth-checker.info	Amazon	10/3/2024	Verified
http://www.bankofamerica-alerts.org	Bank of America	10/4/2024	Verified

4.2.4   Federated Learning for Threat Intelligence Sharing

Today's computing paradigms are significantly shifting toward distributed computing, where a network of nodes communicates with each other. To make such a system robust against risks and hazards, such as cyber attacks, it is essential for each node to share its knowledge and experiences that is known as threat intelligence with other nodes.

The growing complexity of cyber threats has led to an increased focus on threat intelligence sharing in distributed computing environments. Threat intelligence involves evidence-based knowledge about threats that can inform decision-making [17]. To address challenges in Industry 4.0 systems, a new threat intelligence scheme using beta mixture-hidden Markov models has been proposed for detecting anomalies in both physical and network systems. Trust and responsible use of sensitive information are crucial for effective threat intelligence sharing. A distributed security framework using blockchain technology has been developed to enhance trust and enable auditing of threat intelligence provenance [18]. To incentivize sharing and overcome reluctance among organizations, a blockchain-based marketplace for cybersecurity threat intelligence has been proposed, using standards like structured threat information expression (STIX) and introducing a cyber threat intelligence (CTI) token as a digital asset.

4.2.4.1   Overview

Traditional threat intelligence methods often involve centralized collection and analysis of data, which, while effective to some extent, raise profound concerns about privacy, scalability, and real-time adaptability. FL, on the other hand, reimagines how intelligence can be shared and utilized by allowing organizations to collaboratively learn from distributed datasets without ever transferring sensitive information to a centralized hub.

The dynamic and decentralized nature of FL ensures that critical threat data, such as indicators of compromise (IoCs) or behavioral patterns of malicious actors, remains securely localized within each organization's infrastructure. This approach not only protects proprietary and confidential data but also significantly reduces the risks of breaches during transmission. FL achieves this by sending model updates instead of raw data, which are then aggregated securely to improve the global model.

One of the most impressive features of FL in this domain is its adaptability to diverse environments. Each participating node—be it a financial institution, healthcare provider, or government entity—can contribute insights based on its unique threat landscape, enhancing the richness and diversity of the intelligence. This makes the global model far more robust and inclusive, capturing an extraordinary array of attack vectors and patterns that would otherwise be unavailable in a centralized approach [19].

A prominent use case involves detecting advanced persistent threats (APTs), which often require deep collaboration across industries to uncover their intricate and stealthy techniques. For instance, financial institutions in different countries could use FL to collectively identify emerging phishing or ransomware campaigns targeting their sector. By sharing encrypted model updates reflecting suspicious activity, these organizations could preemptively bolster their defenses without exposing sensitive customer data (Fig. 4.5).

Another awe-inspiring application is in enhancing the detection of zero-day exploits. FL enables organizations to share learnings from newly identified vulnerabilities almost instantaneously. For example, when a novel malware strain targeting IoT devices emerges, FL allows different entities managing IoT ecosystems to collaboratively train a model that detects this malware based on diverse environmental signals, thereby accelerating the time to mitigation.

4.2.4.2 Implementation

FL's foundational principle of keeping raw data localized is critical in threat intelligence, where sharing sensitive information—such as internal logs, behavioral patterns, or threat signatures—can pose risks to privacy, compliance, and competitive advantage. Encryption techniques, such as secure multi-party computation (SMPC) or homomorphic encryption, play a key role in protecting model updates during their transmission to the global server.

The diversity of data sources in threat intelligence, such as endpoint logs, network traffic, or email metadata, requires FL systems to accommodate heterogeneous data formats and distributions. Moreover, organizations in different industries face distinct types of cyber threats, necessitating personalization techniques like meta-learning or transfer learning to ensure the global model adapts effectively to local needs.

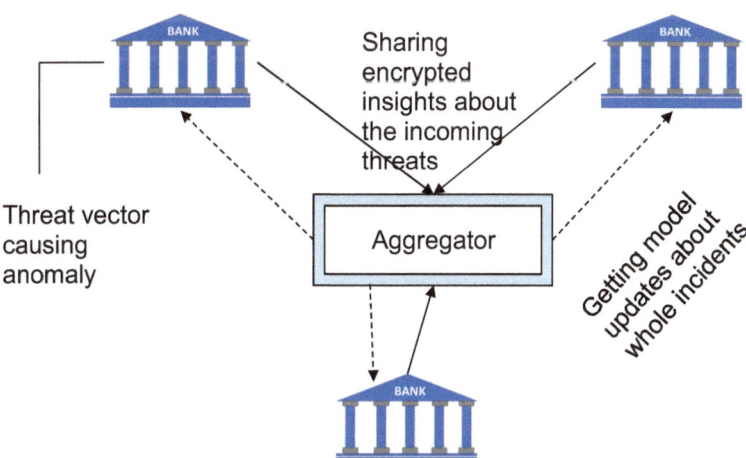

Fig. 4.5 General FL-based threat intelligence sharing in banking systems

A fundamental challenge in FL is ensuring that the aggregated global model effectively represents the diverse patterns and insights contributed by all participants. Techniques such as Federated Averaging (FedAvg) or alternative aggregation algorithms like robust federated learning can be tailored to handle malicious contributions such as poisoned updates in the context of cybersecurity.

Threat intelligence sharing often involves global networks with numerous participants, from enterprises to government agencies. Communication-efficient FL methods, such as quantized updates, sparse representation, or periodic model updates, are essential to ensure scalability and reduce bandwidth consumption.

4.2.4.3   Federated Learning Architectures for Threat Intelligence Sharing

Inspiring from common FL architectures, one can adapt them for threat intelligence sharing as well.

4.2.4.3.1   Hierarchical Federated Learning

Hierarchical Federated Learning organizes participants into clusters based on shared characteristics, such as geographic location or industry type. Within each cluster, local models are trained and aggregated, and the aggregated results are then used for global updates. This approach is particularly effective for scaling systems with a large number of participants by reducing communication overhead. Additionally, it enhances model specialization by allowing localized adaptations, which is beneficial for addressing region-specific threats like localized phishing campaigns or malware variants [20]. However, the clustering process can introduce complexities, as the grouping needs to balance similarities in data with diversity for robust learning. The additional clustering step can also delay updates, which might be a concern in environments requiring real-time threat mitigation. For instance, in a smart city deployment, clusters could represent specific city zones, each analyzing cyber threats to IoT devices and aggregating insights at a city-wide level.

4.2.4.3.2   Cross-Silo Federated Learning

Cross-silo Federated Learning involves a small and fixed number of trusted participants, such as enterprises, research institutions, or government agencies. These participants collaborate to train a global model without exposing their sensitive data, often operating within highly regulated industries like healthcare or finance. This architecture is advantageous because the data from participants is typically well-organized, offering high-quality insights into specific types of cyber threats. It also ensures compliance with data privacy regulations, such as GDPR, as raw data never leaves the silo [21]. However, the limited number of participants may restrict the diversity of the data, which could hinder the model's generalizability to broader threat landscapes. An example of this application is in threat intelligence sharing among national cybersecurity agencies, where each agency shares updates from its malware analysis efforts to collaboratively strengthen a global model detecting state-sponsored attacks.

4.2.4.3.3 Cross-Device Federated Learning

Cross-device Federated Learning is designed for large-scale collaboration across numerous lightweight devices, such as IoT sensors, firewalls, and mobile devices. Each device trains models locally and contributes updates to a global model. This approach excels in scalability, as it can support thousands or even millions of devices, each contributing to a richer and more diverse model. It also enables real-time threat detection, as edge devices can act immediately upon detecting anomalies, such as malware exploiting an IoT sensor. However, the resource limitations of these devices, including constrained computation power and memory, can restrict the complexity of the models they can train. Connectivity issues and power constraints further challenge consistent participation [22]. In smart grids, cross-device FL enables IoT-enabled power meters and other devices to collaboratively detect malware trying to disrupt energy distribution while adapting to localized attack vectors.

4.2.4.3.4 Federated Transfer Learning

Federated Transfer Learning facilitates collaboration among participants with non-overlapping datasets or feature spaces. It is particularly useful when participants belong to different industries with distinct threat landscapes but can still benefit from shared insights. For example, a technology firm focusing on malware detection can collaborate with a financial organization specializing in phishing detection. Through federated transfer learning, both parties can enhance their models by sharing domain-specific knowledge without compromising data privacy [23]. This architecture is advantageous for domain adaptability, as it allows learning across diverse datasets while requiring less shared data. However, it requires sophisticated techniques to align feature spaces across domains, which can introduce additional complexity. An example application could involve a multinational threat intelligence system where insights about phishing campaigns in the financial sector are transferred to technology firms, enabling them to detect multi-vector attacks that combine phishing with malware delivery (Table 4.7).

4.2.4.4 Discussion on Benefits

The enhanced detection of multi-vector attacks is made possible by combining insights from different sectors, enabling the identification of complex threats like phishing, malware, and ransomware. For instance, an advanced persistent threat

Table 4.7 Comparison of different FL architectures

Feature	Hierarchical FL	Cross-Silo FL	Cross-device FL	Federated transfer learning
Scalability	Moderate	Low	High	Low
Diversity of data	Moderate	Low	High	High
Privacy protection	Strong	Strong	Moderate	Strong
Model specialization	High (within clusters)	High	Low	Moderate
Communication efficiency	High (within clusters)	Moderate	Low	Moderate
Complexity	Moderate	Low	High	High
Best use case	Regional or industry-specific threats	Highly regulated industries	IoT and edge-based systems	Domain-specific knowledge transfer

(APT) group targeting energy companies with phishing emails that lead to ransomware deployment can be detected through shared intelligence from both the banking and energy sectors. Federated Learning preserves privacy by ensuring that sensitive data, such as financial transactions or patient records, remains within the organization, addressing concerns and meeting regulatory requirements like GDPR and HIPAA. Additionally, FL facilitates cross-sector collaboration, breaking down sector-specific silos and enabling the sharing of threat intelligence. This allows emerging attack vectors identified in one sector to preemptively inform defenses in another, fostering a unified and proactive cybersecurity front.

4.3 Conclusion

FL addresses key challenges faced by traditional machine learning methods in cybersecurity by preserving data privacy, enhancing scalability, and enabling continuous learning. This decentralized approach allows organizations to collaborate on improving threat detection and mitigation without compromising sensitive data, a crucial aspect in today's privacy-focused world. As the cyber threat landscape grows increasingly sophisticated, FL-based systems provide a way to enhance the resilience and adaptability of defense mechanisms, making them more effective against emerging threats.

Looking ahead, the potential of FL extends beyond current applications. For instance, FL could enable cross-border collaboration for critical infrastructure protection, where power grids in different countries share insights to preempt and defend against cyberattacks without revealing sensitive operational data. In smart cities, FL could allow decentralized learning between IoT devices in transportation systems, ensuring they collectively detect and respond to anomalies such as hacking attempts on traffic control systems. Furthermore, FL might revolutionize threat response in space communications, where satellites could share attack signatures while keeping sensitive telemetry data secure. These possibilities highlight FL's capacity to not only strengthen cybersecurity but also enable innovative solutions tailored to future technological advancements.

References

1. Folino, F., Folino, G., Pisani, F. S., Sabatino, P., & Pontieri, L. (2024, March). A scalable vertical federated learning framework for analytics in the cybersecurity domain. In *2024 32nd Euromicro international conference on Parallel, Distributed and Network-Based Processing (PDP)* (pp. 245–252). IEEE.
2. Thantharate, P., & Anurag, T. (2023, December). CYBRIA-pioneering federated learning for privacy-aware cybersecurity with brilliance. In *2023 IEEE 20th international conference on smart communities: Improving quality of life using AI, robotics and IoT (HONET)* (pp. 56–61). IEEE.
3. Li, S. C., Chen, Y. W., & Huang, Y. (2021). Examining compliance with personal data protection regulations in interorganizational data analysis. *Sustainability, 13*(20), 11459.
4. Verbraeken, J., Wolting, M., Katzy, J., Kloppenburg, J., Verbelen, T., & Rellermeyer, J. S. (2020). A survey on distributed machine learning. *ACM Computing Surveys (CSUR), 53*(2), 1–33.
5. Böse, B., Avasarala, B., Tirthapura, S., Chung, Y. Y., & Steiner, D. (2017). Detecting insider threats using radish: A system for real-time anomaly detection in heterogeneous data streams. *IEEE Systems Journal, 11*(2), 471–482.
6. Sarhan, M., Layeghy, S., Moustafa, N., & Portmann, M. (2023). Cyber threat intelligence sharing scheme based on federated learning for network intrusion detection. *Journal of Network and Systems Management, 31*(1), 3.
7. Ashoor, A. S., & Gore, S. (2011). Importance of intrusion detection system (IDS). *International Journal of Scientific and Engineering Research, 2*(1), 1–4.
8. Garcia-Teodoro, P., Diaz-Verdejo, J., Maciá-Fernández, G., & Vázquez, E. (2009). Anomaly-based network intrusion detection: Techniques, systems and challenges. *Computers & Security, 28*(1–2), 18–28.
9. Sarhan, M., Layeghy, S., & Portmann, M. (2021). Feature analysis for machine learning-based IoT intrusion detection. *arXiv preprint*, arXiv:2108.12732.
10. Rey, V., Sánchez, P. M. S., Celdrán, A. H., & Bovet, G. (2022). Federated learning for malware detection in IoT devices. *Comput Netw, 204*, 108693.
11. Santos, I., Penya, Y. K., Devesa, J., & Bringas, P. G. (2009, May). N-grams-based file signatures for malware detection. In *International conference on enterprise information systems* (Vol. 1, pp. 317–320). SCITEPRESS.
12. Fukushima, Y., Sakai, A., Hori, Y., & Sakurai, K. (2010, October). A behavior based malware detection scheme for avoiding false positive. In *2010 6th IEEE workshop on secure network protocols* (pp. 79–84). IEEE.
13. Singh, J., & Singh, J. (2021). A survey on machine learning-based malware detection in executable files. *Journal of Systems Architecture, 112*, 101861.
14. Rahman, S. A., Tout, H., Talhi, C., & Mourad, A. (2020). Internet of Things intrusion detection: Centralized, on-device, or federated learning? *IEEE Network, 34*, 310–317.
15. Alani, M. M., & Tawfik, H. (2022). PhishNot: A cloud-based machine-learning approach to phishing URL detection. *Computer Networks, 218*, 109407.
16. Zeng, V., Baki, S., Aassal, A. E., Verma, R., De Moraes, L. F. T., & Das, A. (2020, March). Diverse datasets and a customizable benchmarking framework for phishing. In *Proceedings of the sixth international workshop on security and privacy analytics* (pp. 35–41).

17. Tounsi, W., & Rais, H. (2018). A survey on technical threat intelligence in the age of sophisticated cyber attacks. *Computers & Security, 72*, 212–233.
18. Preuveneers, D., Joosen, W., Bernal Bernabe, J., & Skarmeta, A. (2020). Distributed security framework for reliable threat intelligence sharing. *Security and Communication Networks, 2020*(1), 8833765.
19. Alazab, M., Swarna Priya, R. M., Parimala, M., Maddikunta, P. K. R., Gadekallu, T. R., & Pham, Q. V. (2021). Federated learning for cybersecurity: Concepts, challenges, and future directions. *IEEE Transactions on Industrial Informatics, 18*(5), 3501–3509.
20. Briggs, C., Fan, Z., & Andras, P. (2020, July). Federated learning with hierarchical clustering of local updates to improve training on non-IID data. In *2020 International Joint Conference on Neural Networks (IJCNN)* (pp. 1–9). IEEE.
21. Huang, C., Huang, J., & Liu, X. (2022). Cross-silo federated learning: Challenges and opportunities. *arXiv preprint*, arXiv:2206.12949.
22. Imteaj, A., Thakker, U., Wang, S., Li, J., & Amini, M. H. (2021). A survey on federated learning for resource-constrained IoT devices. *IEEE Internet of Things Journal, 9*(1), 1–24.
23. Saha, S., & Ahmad, T. (2021). Federated transfer learning: Concept and applications. *Intelligenza Artificiale, 15*(1), 35–44.

Chapter 5
Closing Thoughts, and Future Directions in Federated Cyber Intelligence

5.1 Introduction

This book explores the fundamental ideas of federated learning, its essential techniques, and its application in cybersecurity. We examined how federated systems might improve intelligent cybersecurity systems by reconciling data privacy requirements with collaborative learning. In this book, both federated learning and cybersecurity are explored over their major characteristics. Chapter 1 introduced the foundational concepts of federated learning, explaining its essence and its potential to enable collaborative intelligence while preserving data privacy. Chapter 2 explored deeper into the technical underpinnings, covering the architecture, communication protocols, and strategies that shape federated learning systems. In light of this, Chap. 3 examined the principles and challenges of cybersecurity. It highlighted the critical role of protecting digital ecosystems in an era of evolving threats. Chapter 4 brought these domains together, showcasing how federated learning can be applied to build intelligent cybersecurity systems. This will enable collaborative threat detection and addressing data privacy concerns. Now, in Chap. 5, we reflect on these discussions, summarizing key insights and envisioning the future of federated cyber intelligence by identifying challenges, emerging trends, and potential research directions.

5.2 Evolution of Federated Learning in Cybersecurity

As organizations face increasing threats and need privacy-preserving solutions, federated learning has emerged as an innovative approach to cybersecurity. This overview highlights recent developments, and the importance of these models in cybersecurity. Federated learning is a machine learning paradigm that enables

H. Tabrizchi, A. Aghasi, *Federated Cyber Intelligence*, SpringerBriefs in Computer Science, https://doi.org/10.1007/978-3-031-86592-3_5

multiple entities to collaboratively train models while keeping their data localized. This approach has gained significant traction due to the rising number of cyberattacks, which have surged dramatically over the past decade. Federated Learning's growing adoption is driven by its ability to enhance threat detection capabilities without compromising sensitive information, making it an essential tool in today's data-driven and security-conscious environment [1].

Recent technological advancements in Federated Learning have improved its effectiveness and widened its applicability. Innovations in model aggregation algorithms and the introduction of enhanced privacy techniques, such as differential privacy and secure collaborative computation, have enabled organizations to share insights while maintaining data confidentiality. These advancements are particularly critical in industries like finance and healthcare, where protecting sensitive data is both a legal and ethical imperative.

The practical applications of federated learning demonstrate its revolutionary potential. In the financial sector, banks employ federated learning to detect fraudulent transactions by training local models on their transaction data and aggregating insights to collectively identify new fraud patterns. Similarly, in the healthcare industry, hospitals employ federated learning to enhance cybersecurity against ransomware attacks while preserving patient privacy. By sharing only model updates instead of raw data, hospitals ensure data confidentiality even as they collaboratively improve their defenses. In telecommunications, service providers use federated learning to collaboratively detect distributed denial of service attacks. This approach allows them to pool threat intelligence without exposing sensitive network traffic, ensuring secure and effective collaboration.

The integration of federated learning into cybersecurity systems has revealed several valuable lessons. One of the most significant is its ability to enhance threat detection by pooling diverse datasets from multiple organizations. This leads to a more comprehensive understanding of emerging threats. By keeping sensitive data localized, federated learning mitigates the risks associated with data breaches during transmission, making it a safer alternative to traditional centralized models. Additionally, its collaborative framework enables organizations to share threat intelligence without compromising competitive advantages or exposing critical data. In this way, cyber adversaries are able to face a united front against them [1, 2].

Federated learning is rising to recognition as a vital solution to security and privacy concerns in cybersecurity. Its collaborative essence eliminates single points of failure by distributing data processing across multiple nodes. This makes it significantly harder for attackers to compromise entire datasets. The collaborative essence of federated learning also enables models to adapt quickly to emerging threats through continuous learning from diverse sources. This enhances their resilience against cyberattacks.

Given all mentioned here, it is undeniable that federated learning represents a significant advancement in cybersecurity strategies. By facilitating collaboration while preserving privacy, it addresses critical cyber security challenges. As organizations increasingly adopt this approach, ongoing research and standardization efforts will be essential to unlocking its full potential across various industries.

Through its unique combination of privacy preservation, collaborative learning, and adaptability, these concepts can play a pivotal role in the future of cybersecurity.

5.3 Federated Learning and Emerging Threats in Cybersecurity

The cybersecurity landscape is undergoing rapid transformation as new and increasingly complicated threats emerge. The advent of technologies such as Internet of Things (IoT), cloud computing, and 5G networks has exponentially increased the attack surface, exposing critical systems to a wider array of vulnerabilities. Traditional security methods often struggle to keep up with this pace due to centralized processing limitations and the inability to respond properly to threats. Federated learning can provide a privacy-preserving solution to these challenges by enabling organizations to collaborate on model training without sharing sensitive data [3, 4].

Cyber threats are becoming more complex, driven by technological advancements and system interconnectedness. Advanced Persistent Threats (APTs), which involve prolonged and targeted cyberattacks, exemplify this sophistication, often leveraging multi-stage intrusion tactics that evade traditional defenses. In addition, the integration of machine learning (ML) by adversaries enables the dynamic evolution of malware through polymorphic techniques, rendering detection systems obsolete without continuous updates. One notable trend is that cybercriminals are using artificial intelligence (AI) to enhance their offensive capabilities. AI is employed to automate vulnerability identification and craft highly targeted phishing campaigns, making attacks both more efficient and more difficult to detect [4].

Through localizing data and enabling collaboration, FL minimizes data breaches risk during transmission. Unlike traditional centralized models, FL ensures that raw data remains on-premise while only model parameters are shared, significantly reducing exposure points during data exchange. This approach is fortified through techniques such as differential privacy and secure aggregation, which add mathematical guarantees against data inference attacks. This framework preserves privacy and enhances the ability to detect and respond to novel threats. Through continuous learning, FL aggregates insights from diverse datasets, allowing real-time model updates. For example, healthcare institutions can employ FL to collaboratively train models that detect ransomware-specific behaviors without exposing patient data, illustrating the real-world impact of this methodology. This capability is particularly crucial for identifying zero-day exploits and previously unknown vulnerabilities. Furthermore, FL enhances anomaly detection by pooling data from multiple sources to identify unusual patterns indicative of cyber threats [3].

Federated Learning's cybersecurity applications are vast and impactful. In the financial sector, FL can mitigate fraud detection challenges by enabling banks to share threat intelligence securely. This leads to improved identification of suspicious transactions. Similarly, telecommunication networks can leverage FL for distributed intrusion detection, ensuring rapid identification of Distributed Denial of Service (DDoS) attacks without compromising user privacy. Autonomous systems, including self-driving cars, also benefit from FL by enabling secure sharing of cybersecurity insights to counter adversarial attacks targeting vehicle control systems [4].

In conclusion, federated learning represents a transformative advancement in addressing the increasingly sophisticated cyber threat landscape. Its effectiveness lies in combining the strengths of decentralized learning architectures with privacy-preserving technologies, ensuring scalability and security. Future research directions include enhancing robustness against adversarial poisoning of models and integrating quantum-safe cryptographic techniques to secure FL frameworks. By fostering collaborative intelligence while preserving data privacy, FL offers a robust framework for countering modern cybersecurity risks. Its adaptability, real-time learning capabilities, and decentralized approach position it as a vital tool for organizational resilience. As threats continue to evolve, Federated Learning will undoubtedly play a pivotal role in shaping the future of cybersecurity strategies across industries.

5.4 Current Challenges in Federated Learning for Cybersecurity

Despite federated learning's potential for enhancing cybersecurity, a number of challenges prevent its effective implementation. The discussion focuses on model poisoning attacks, adversarial robustness, heterogeneity of data, scalability issues, privacy concerns, and interoperability, communication overhead, regulatory and ethical barriers, and limited standardization.

5.4.1 Data Heterogeneity

Data heterogeneity poses a significant challenge in FL, as data quality and quantity vary widely across participating organizations. This non-IID (independent and identically distributed) nature of data can lead to performance degradation and convergence issues during model training. If one client's data is significantly different from others, it may disproportionately influence the global model, resulting in poor generalization across diverse datasets. Additionally, skewed datasets may amplify biases in predictions, particularly in cybersecurity tasks such as threat detection or malware classification, where data imbalance is common. For example, systems in developed regions may exhibit different threat signatures than those in developing regions, limiting the FL model's general applicability.

Addressing data heterogeneity requires innovative algorithms capable of handling diverse data distributions effectively. Strategies such as statistical averaging and personalized federated learning have been proposed to improve model performance under heterogeneous conditions. Techniques like Federated Averaging with adaptive weights and hierarchical FL structures are being explored to better balance contributions from diverse clients. This is done while reducing the negative impact of outlier datasets.

5.4.2   Scalability Issues

As FL networks grow in size, scalability becomes a critical concern. The computational overhead associated with training models on numerous devices can lead to significant communication bottlenecks during the aggregation phase. Furthermore, the limited bandwidth in edge computing environments exacerbates these challenges, as devices in remote or resource-constrained locations may struggle to participate in high-frequency communication rounds. Efficient resource management and optimization techniques are necessary to ensure large-scale FL systems operate smoothly without overwhelming network resources. Emerging solutions include gradient compression, decentralized aggregation, and asynchronous FL frameworks, which minimize communication overhead while maintaining model accuracy.

5.4.3   Privacy Concerns

Despite its privacy-preserving capabilities, FL is not immune to privacy risks. Model inversion attacks can expose sensitive information through shared gradients or model updates. Attackers may reconstruct aspects of the original data by analyzing these updates, risking user privacy. Additionally, membership inference attacks threaten FL by determining whether a specific data point was part of the training dataset. This is especially critical in applications such as healthcare cybersecurity, where sensitive patient data is involved.

To counteract these threats, techniques like differential privacy can be employed to add noise to model updates. This makes it more challenging for adversaries to extract useful information while still allowing for effective learning. Other approaches include homomorphic encryption, which ensures that computations on encrypted data are performed without decryption. In addition, secure multi-party computation (SMPC), which facilitates secure aggregation of contributions from multiple clients.

5.4.4   Interoperability and Standardization

The lack of uniform protocols and frameworks for implementing FL in cybersecurity systems presents another challenge. Without standardized approaches, integrating FL into existing cybersecurity infrastructures can be complex and inconsistent across different platforms and organizations. This lack of standardization also leads to discrepancies in threat intelligence sharing across industries, reducing FL systems' collaborative efficacy. The absence of a unified taxonomy for FL-related metrics and performance benchmarks further hinders the evaluation and comparison of FL solutions in diverse environments.

Establishing common standards will facilitate smoother deployment and enhance collaboration among various stakeholders involved in federated learning initiatives. Industry-led efforts, such as the IEEE's development of federated AI standards, show promise in addressing these concerns. Collaborative efforts between academia and international regulatory bodies will also be crucial for creating globally accepted guidelines.

5.4.5   Communication Overhead

High bandwidth usage during model updates in large-scale FL networks is a bottleneck for widespread implementation. As FL networks grow, frequent transmission of model updates (gradients or parameters) places a heavy load on network resources. Edge devices with limited bandwidth or unstable connections—such as IoT devices—struggle to keep up, leading to participation drops or delays in aggregation.

Solutions such as gradient compression (e.g., sparsification or quantization) and asynchronous updates have been proposed to mitigate this. Additionally, decentralized aggregation approaches, such as Gossip Learning, offer promising alternatives by reducing reliance on a central server, but further research is needed to optimize their efficiency in real-world cybersecurity applications.

5.4.6   Regulatory and Ethical Barriers

Differing regulations on data sharing across regions (e.g., GDPR vs. local laws) complicate FL deployment. For instance, while the EU's GDPR emphasizes strict control over personal data, other jurisdictions may have laxer or conflicting regulations, making cross-border collaboration challenging. Organizations must navigate these variations while ensuring that FL frameworks remain compliant and privacy-preserving.

Ethical concerns, such as biases introduced during FL training due to unequal representation of global datasets, further compound these barriers. Ethical AI frameworks, coupled with region-specific FL customization, can help mitigate these issues, but balancing privacy, compliance, and fairness remains an ongoing challenge.

5.4.7   Limited Standardization

The absence of universal frameworks for secure and efficient FL implementation hinders scalability and adoption. For instance, cybersecurity applications involving threat intelligence sharing across organizations lack consistent standards for model updates, encryption protocols, and communication interfaces. This gap limits interoperability and increases the risk of integration failures in multi-stakeholder environments.

Efforts like the IEEE's federated AI standardization initiatives aim to address these challenges. However, widespread adoption requires collaboration across industry, academia, and government to ensure that such standards are robust, future-proof, and applicable across diverse use cases.

While federated learning holds great promise for advancing cybersecurity, continuous research in secure aggregation, robust anomaly detection, and privacy-preserving methods will drive the evolution of FL in combating cyber threats. Additionally, fostering industry-wide collaborations and regulatory frameworks will ensure the scalability and reliability of FL systems. Ongoing research and development efforts will be essential to create robust solutions that enhance the efficacy and reliability of FL in combating emerging cybersecurity threats.

5.5   Future Directions in Federated Cyber Intelligence

As the cybersecurity landscape evolves, the integration of federated learning into cyber intelligence systems is becoming more and more crucial. This section outlines future directions for federated cyber intelligence. It focuses on the synergies between FL and AI, the potential of edge computing, the intersection of blockchain technology, advancements in privacy-preserving techniques, trust frameworks, collaborative platforms, and cross-disciplinary collaborations. In the future, robust, resilient, and adaptive cybersecurity systems will be made possible by these advancements.

5.5.1   AI and Federated Learning Synergies

Combining federated learning with other artificial intelligence techniques can significantly enhance cybersecurity solutions. Through an integration of federated
learning and reinforcement learning, systems can learn optimal strategies for threat
detection and response in real time based on real-time feedback from their environment. For instance, reinforcement learning could allow federated learning models to
simulate various cyberattack scenarios, iteratively improving their responses to
upcoming and evolving threats. Such systems could predict and prevent cyberattacks with enhanced accuracy over time. This dynamic learning process can improve
security measures' effectiveness by continuously optimizing them against evolving
threats. Aside from this, as a result of the use of adversarial AI techniques it is possible to develop more robust federated learning models that can withstand attempts
to manipulate or compromise them, so that they can develop more robust federated
learning models. Adversarial Training, where federated learning models are inten-
tionally exposed to adversarial inputs during training, has shown promise in enhancing robustness. This approach is especially critical for detecting stealthy attacks,
such as advanced persistent threats, that aim to exploit latent vulnerabilities. By
training models to recognize and counteract adversarial inputs, organizations can
enhance their defenses against sophisticated attacks. In addition to this, the combination of federated learning and anomaly detection algorithms can identify unusual
patterns indicative of cyber threats. When integrated with deep learning methods
like autoencoders or Gaussian Mixture Models, federated learning enables precise
detection of anomalies across distributed datasets. This includes identifying irregu-
lar traffic in a network or spotting unusual login patterns. This can lead to a quicker
identification and mitigation of threats by combining disparate data from different
sources.

5.5.2   Edge Computing and Federated Learning

The integration of federated learning with edge computing presents exciting opportunities for real-time, localized threat detection and prevention.

Localized processing in edge computing environments reduces latency and
improves response times by processing data closer to its source. This is particularly
critical in IoT networks, where real-time processing is essential for preventing cas-
cading failures caused by compromised devices. Federated learning enables devices
at the edge to collaboratively learn from localized data without transmitting sensitive information to centralized servers. In addition to the detection of large quanti-
ties of threats, edge computing combined with federated learning can provide
scalable solutions that can handle vast amounts of data while maintaining privacy. It
enables cost-efficient, decentralized cybersecurity by reducing reliance on cloud
infrastructures. Through interconnected IoT systems, edge-based federated learning

can enhance the detection of physical security breaches in industries such as smart cities.

5.5.3 Blockchain and Federated Learning

The intersection of blockchain technology and federated learning offers a framework for secure, transparent, and verifiable cybersecurity model training. The blockchain can provide an immutable ledger for tracking model updates and contributions across nodes in a federated learning network. As a result of this traceability, anomalies, such as malicious updates or inconsistencies, can be identified and audited quickly. As well as strengthening the integrity of federated learning systems, blockchain can be used for decentralized authentication mechanisms. The blockchain mitigates risks such as malicious devices injecting poisoned data into the network by ensuring that only verified nodes can participate. This is critical for federated frameworks operating in high-stakes environments like national defense.

5.5.4 Advancing Privacy-Preserving Techniques

Advanced privacy-preserving techniques are crucial for securing federated learning systems and ensuring their long-term sustainability. Data noise is added to data during model training by differential privacy. This method prevents sensitive information about users or organizations from being inferred from aggregated results and has already demonstrated its effectiveness in anomaly detection within distributed logs while maintaining privacy. In addition to differential privacy, homomorphic encryption further strengthens security by enabling computations on encrypted data without requiring decryption. When these techniques are combined, they create a robust, multi-layered defense against inference attacks. For instance, this combination allows encrypted malware signatures to be compared across systems, enabling collaborative threat detection while safeguarding sensitive data. By preserving privacy in such scenarios, homomorphic encryption complements differential privacy and ensures effective model training. However, as quantum computing continues to advance, FL systems face new threats, making quantum-safe algorithms increasingly essential. Techniques such as lattice-based encryption are emerging as vital solutions for securing FL frameworks against quantum attacks. To address these evolving challenges, research into post-quantum cryptographic methods remains critical for ensuring the long-term security and resilience of federated learning systems.

5.5.5 Building Trust Frameworks

Establishing trust frameworks is essential for fostering collaboration in federated learning environments, enabling secure and reliable participation across diverse stakeholders. Decentralized authentication, facilitated by blockchain technology, ensures that all participants in the network are verified and trustworthy. This approach is particularly advantageous in cross-border cybersecurity activities, where cross-border trust can be established through transparent verification mechanisms. Additionally, implementing transparent auditing mechanisms through blockchain enhances accountability by providing visibility into each participant's contributions to the federated learning process. In addition to improving confidence in the overall system, these audits establish a culture of trust and collaboration.

5.5.6 Collaborative Threat Intelligence Platforms

The development of global-scale collaborative platforms is crucial for enabling secure sharing of cyber threat intelligence across organizations, resulting in a unified approach to cybersecurity. These platforms facilitate secure data sharing while ensuring compliance with data protection regulations. For example, federated learning-enabled platforms allow financial institutions to detect global fraud patterns without compromising proprietary or customer data. Moreover, they support collective defense strategies by enabling organizations to pool knowledge about emerging threats. This collaborative approach enhances the ability to identify zero-day vulnerabilities efficiently, promoting proactive and robust cyber defense strategies that benefit all participants.

5.5.7 Collaborative Threat Intelligence

The development of global-scale collaborative platforms is crucial for enabling secure sharing of cyber threat intelligence across organizations, fostering a unified approach to cybersecurity. These platforms facilitate secure data sharing while ensuring compliance with data protection regulations. For example, federated learning-enabled platforms allow financial institutions to detect global fraud patterns without compromising proprietary or customer data. Moreover, they support collective defense strategies by enabling organizations to pool knowledge about emerging threats. This collaborative approach enhances the ability to identify zero-day vulnerabilities efficiently, promoting proactive and robust cyber defense strategies that benefit all participants.

5.5.8   Cross-Disciplinary Collaborations

Cross-disciplinary collaborations between academia, industry, and government entities are essential for addressing federated learning challenges and driving its adoption in cybersecurity. Collaborative research initiatives can foster innovation in developing federated learning methodologies specifically tailored for cybersecurity applications, with joint funding supporting solutions to complex issues such as protecting federated models against sophisticated threats like insider attacks. Additionally, engaging policymakers in discussions about standardization and best practices is vital for establishing a cohesive framework that facilitates widespread adoption. Harmonizing international data-sharing laws will be particularly critical in unlocking the full potential of FL for global cybersecurity initiatives.

5.6   Conclusion

The closing chapter of this book underscores the transformative potential of federated learning in addressing key cybersecurity issues. While its application has shown significant promise in mitigating privacy risks and enabling distributed threat intelligence, federated learning still faces limitations such as data heterogeneity, adversarial attacks, and resource constraints. To realize its full potential, future efforts must focus on developing resilient algorithms, improving scalability, and creating collaboration among academia, industry, and policymakers. By addressing these challenges, federated cyber intelligence can evolve into a cornerstone of modern cybersecurity. This will provide a safer and more secure digital landscape for the future.

References

1. Ghimire, B., & Rawat, D. B. (2022). Recent advances on federated learning for cybersecurity and cybersecurity for federated learning for internet of things. *IEEE Internet of Things Journal, 9*(11), 8229–8249.
2. Alazab, M., Swarna Priya, R. M., Parimala, M., Maddikunta, P. K. R., Gadekallu, T. R., & Pham, Q. V. (2021). Federated learning for cybersecurity: Concepts, challenges, and future directions. *IEEE Transactions on Industrial Informatics, 18*(5), 3501–3509.
3. Ferrag, M. A., Friha, O., Maglaras, L., Janicke, H., & Shu, L. (2021). Federated deep learning for cyber security in the internet of things: Concepts, applications, and experimental analysis. *IEEE Access, 9*, 138509–138542.
4. Al Mallah, R., Badu-Marfo, G., & Farooq, B. (2021, July). Cybersecurity threats in connected and automated vehicles based federated learning systems. In *2021 IEEE intelligent vehicles symposium workshops (IV workshops)* (pp. 13–18). IEEE.